SCOTTISH
LOCH & CANAL
STEAMERS

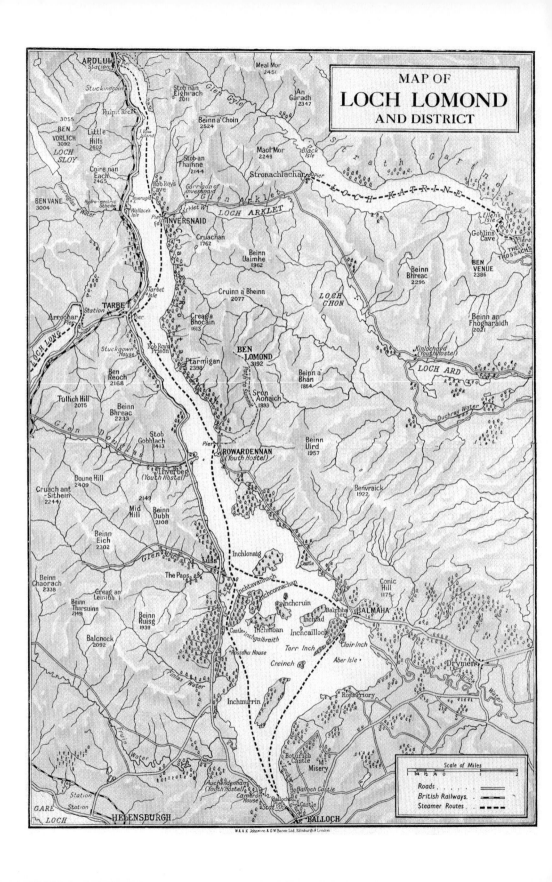

MAP OF
LOCH LOMOND
AND DISTRICT

Scale of Miles

Roads . . . .
British Railways . . . . .
Steamer Routes . . . .

W & A K Johnston & G W Bacon Ltd. Edinburgh & London

SCOTTISH LOCH & CANAL STEAMERS

ALISTAIR DEAYTON

TEMPUS

Frontispiece: A map of the steamer service on Loch Lomond from the 1955 timetable.

First published 2004

Tempus Publishing Limited
The Mill, Brimscombe Port,
Stroud, Gloucestershire, GL5 2QG
www.tempus-publishing.com

British Library Cataloguing in Publication Data.
A catalogue record for this book is available from the British Library.

ISBN 0 7524 3170 6

Typesetting and origination by Tempus Publishing Limited.
Printed in Great Britain by Midway Colour Print, Wiltshire.

Contents

Introduction

The inland lochs of Scotland have seen a wide variety of passenger steamers and motor vessels since the very dawn of steam navigation. Tourism has always been important in some of these, since the publication of Sir Walter Scott's *The Lady of the Lake* in 1810. Other lochs have seen steamers make up an essential part of the local transport network, especially prior to the building of modern roads. Scotland's four major canals – the Forth and Clyde, Union, Crinan, and Caledonian – have all seen steamer or motor vessel operations, with those on the Forth and Clyde dating back to the earliest years of steam propulsion.

Loch Lomond
Steamer services started early on Loch Lomond in 1817 with *Marion*, and the Loch Lomond Steam Boat Company was formed in 1825. After various changes of ownership and name, the North British Steam Packet Co. took it over in 1888. In 1896, the Dumbarton and Balloch Joint Line Committee, which was jointly owned by the North British, Lanarkshire and Dumbartonshire and Caledonian Railways, took over the Dumbarton to Balloch railway and the loch steamers. In 1909 the Lanarkshire and Dumbartonshire Railway was taken over by the Caledonian Railway, and in 1923 joint ownership passed to the London, Midland & Scottish and London & North Eastern Railways. In 1948 it passed to the British Transport Commission, and to the Caledonian Steam Packet in 1953. In 1969, *Maid of the Loch* became part of the Scottish Transport Group, and was owned for a while by the bus operator W. Alexander & Sons (Midland) Ltd, while still managed by the Caledonian Steam Packet Co. Ltd. In 1973 she passed to Caledonian MacBrayne. In March 1982 Ind Coope Alloa Brewery Ltd purchased her, followed in 1989 with joint ownership by James Fisher & Sons of Barrow-in-Furness and the Sea Management Company of Queensland. However, the latter went bankrupt the following year and ownership passed to the Francis Hotel Group of Newcastle. In 1992 they also got into financial difficulties and Dumbarton District Council took a hand in keeping her afloat.

The steamer service on Loch Lomond has maintained a fairly regular pattern over the years, with departures from Balloch and calls at Balmaha, Luss, Rowardennan, Tarbet, Inversnaid and Ardlui. Luss was closed in 1952 and Ardlui in 1963. They were replaced by a cruise to the head of the loch. Balmaha closed in 1971 and Tarbet in 1974, although Luss re-opened in 1980.

Prince Albert, which was built in 1850, was the first steamer to introduce a series of 'Royal' names. She was followed by: *Queen Victoria* in 1852, *Prince of Wales* in 1858, *Prince Consort* in 1862 and *Princess of Wales* in 1866. *Prince Albert* was sold off the Loch in 1862, *Queen Victoria* in 1866, and *Princess of Wales* in 1881. *Prince of Wales* and *Prince Consort* survived until around 1900. *Empress* was built in 1888 and was the last steamer ordered by the Loch Lomond Steam Boat Company. Sisters *Prince George* and *Princess May* followed for the joint committee in 1898 and 1899 respectively, and they were followed by *Prince Edward* in 1912. She was the last steamer to be sailed up the Leven, where she spent over a year before reaching the loch. In 1914, two of the Thames steamers built in 1905 for London County Council, were purchased and became *Princess Patricia* and *Queen Mary*. The former was mainly used on short cruises from Balloch, whilst the latter was seriously damaged by fire shortly after arriving on the loch, and never saw service. *Empress* was broken up in 1933, *Princess Patricia* in 1939 and *Prince George* in 1942.

In 1953, British Railways ordered a new paddle steamer, named *Maid of the Loch*. She was built in sections by A. & J. Inglis on the Clyde and re-erected at Balloch. In hindsight she was too big for the likely passenger demand on the loch. Her advent enabled *Princess May* to be broken up, and *Prince Edward* only lasted until 1955. *Maid of the Loch* continued in service until 1981, and was then laid up at Balloch. The following year *Countess of Kempock* was brought to the loch and served as *Countess Fiona* until 1989, being then left in limbo on the slipway until broken up some ten years later. *Maid of the Loch* has gone through various changes of ownership and is now owned by the preservation group, the Loch Lomond Steamship Co. and operates as a static restaurant and café/bar. There are plans to return her to service but the restoration of the slipway at Balloch, which is necessary for her under-hull painting and renovation, is dependent on lottery funding. Mechanical restoration, including new boilers will also be expensive.

Small boats have operated out of Balloch since the early 1900s, originally steam launches. Since the Second World War there have been a bewildering variety of motorboats and launches used by both Sweeney's, based on the western bank of the River Leven, and Loch Lomond Sailings Ltd, which was later Mullen's, on the eastern back above the road bridge. In 2002 the latter company was taken over by Sweeney's.

MacFarlane's have maintained a year-round mail service from Balmaha to the Loch Lomond Islands since 1948, with the open launches *Marion*, *Margaret* and *Lady Jean*.

Occasional trip boats have operated from Luss, especially during the village's period of fame when it was used as a location for the STV series, *Take the High Road*.

Cruise Loch Lomond has operated loch cruises from Tarbet and Inveruglas from the 1970s onward, with a variety of craft, often in connection with coach tours.

Loch Awe

Steamers were operated on Loch Awe from the early 1860s onwards, with *Queen of the Lake* of 1863 coming into the ownership of David Hutcheson in the early 1870s. She was replaced by *Lochawe* in 1876; the service was from Ford, initially going to the Pass of Brander and, following the opening of the Callander and Oban Railway in 1880, to Lochawe pier, which adjoined the station of the same name. It was part of an alternative route to the sea journey from Crinan to Oban that formed part of the Royal Route. The owner of the Portsonachan Hotel introduced a steamer named *Kilchurn Castle* in 1883, which was followed by *Caledonia* in 1895. In 1882 the Lochawe Hotel, which was adjacent to the station of that name, entered steamer ownership with *Countess of Breadalbane* and the small steam launch *Mona*, which was replaced by another steam launch named *Growley* in around 1900. *Caledonia* was scrapped in 1918 and *Lochawe* did not re-enter service after the First World War. *Countess of Breadalbane* was sold to the Caledonian Steam Packet Co. Ltd in 1922, and was scrapped in 1936 when she was replaced by a motor vessel of the same name. Her saloon still exists in superb condition near Loch Etive. The second *Countess* was moved to Loch Fyne by road in 1952 and had a subsequent career on the Clyde, and ultimately on Loch Lomond as *Countess Fiona*.

In 1986 the steam launch *Lady Rowena* reintroduced passenger services to the loch, and was joined by the motor vessel *Flower of Scotland* in 1990.

Loch Etive

Steamer services were started on this loch in 1877 with *Ben Starav*, which was replaced by *Glenetive* in 1880 and then *Ossian* in 1885. After the Oban to Ballachulish railway was opened, a circular service could be offered – by train from Oban to Ballachulish, coach and horses to Lochetivehead, steamer to Achnacloich and train back to Oban. *Ossian* ceased sailing in 1913. Various motorboats maintained passenger services in the inter-war period, and in 1939 the 'Yacht *Darthula II*', as she was advertised, entered service. After war service, she returned to serve on the loch until 1964, being replaced by *Etive Shearwater* for a couple of years, followed by *Jessie Ellen* in the early 1970s, and the purpose-built *Anne of Etive* which has operated since 1976. Calls at Lochetivehead ceased in the mid-sixties. *Darthula II* remains in existence, most recently serving as a trip boat in Portsmouth harbour, while *Jessie Ellen* was sold for service in Orkney.

Loch Katrine

This loch, featured in Scott's *The Lady of the Lake*, had a passenger service by large rowing boats from the early years of the nineteenth century. A small paddle steamer named *Gipsy* was introduced in 1843, but after only a week's service she disappeared one night. It was believed that rival boatmen had sunk her in the deepest part of the lake. In 1846, another paddle steamer named *Rob Roy* entered service, and she was replaced by a second steamer of the same name in 1855, this time screw propelled. 1900 saw the arrival of *Sir Walter Scott*, which continues in service to this day. Since 1856 Loch Katrine has been the major water supply for the city of Glasgow and, to avoid pollution, *Sir Walter Scott* is fuelled by smokeless fuel. Previously owned by Eglinton Hotels Ltd, who leased the rights to sailings from Glasgow Corporation, in 1952 she was purchased by Glasgow Corporation Water Department. Following various changes in responsibility for public water supplies over the past half-century, she is now owned by Scottish Water.

Loch Shiel

David MacBrayne had an early venture on Loch Shiel from 1893 to 1897, with the steam launch *Maud*. In 1898, the steam launch *Lady of the Lake* entered service, followed in 1899 by *Clanranald*. However, she was of too deep a draught and was replaced by *Clanranald II* in 1900. The latter had her steam engine replaced by diesels in 1926 and was broken up in 1954. The mail service from Glenfinnan to Acharacle, which was maintained by the Loch Shiel Steamboat Service Co. Ltd, was taken over in 1954 by David MacBrayne Ltd. They built the two small motor vessels *Lochshiel* and *Lochailort* for the service. The former was transferred to Iona in 1962 and the latter to Kyle of Lochalsh in 1967, when a road connection replaced the mail service. The open motor launch *Rose Isle* ran excursions from 1968 for a period, as has the motor vessel *Sileas* from around 1999.

Loch Tay

The Loch Tay Steamboat Company was formed in 1882 when the two steamers *Lady of the Lake* and *Sybilla* were built to operate on the loch. The latter was a cargo steamer with a small saloon aft; a similar steamer named *Carlotta* was built in 1883. 1907 saw the arrival of *Queen of the Lake*. The Loch service ran from Loch Tay pier near Killin, which was served by an extension of the Killin branch railway, to Kenmore. The steamers did not operate in 1921 and the company was taken over in 1922 by the Caledonian Steam Packet Co. Ltd. *Lady of the Lake* and *Sybilla* were broken up in 1929 and *Queen of the Lake* was taken out of service at the start of war in 1939, although she was not scrapped until 1950. From 1989 the Croft-na-Caber Hotel near Kenmore has run the small launch *Maid of the Tay* on loch excursions. In 2004, the newly-built steamer *Spirit of the Tay*, built to the same design as the second *Rob Roy* on Loch Katrine, is scheduled to enter service on the Loch from Kenmore.

The Caledonian Canal and Loch Ness

The MacBrayne steamers *Lochness, Gairlochy* and *Glengarry*, which operated on Loch Ness and through the Caledonian Canal to Banavie, are described in *MacBrayne Steamers*. Similarly, there are descriptions of those, such as *Cavalier*, which operated as passenger/cargo services from Glasgow to Inverness.

Modern excursion services on Loch Ness began in 1948 with the converted Fairmile launch *Lenrodian*, which ran for the next two seasons. The motor launch *Cramond Brig* offered a season of excursions in 1958. From 1961, the British Waterways board offered excursions from Inverness with the ice-breaking tug *Scot II*, which had just been converted from steam to diesel. From 1961 to 1966 *Jessie Ellen* offered a competing service. In 1975 Jacobite Cruises commenced services with four motor launches, with two operating out of Inverness and two out of Fort William. The latter service soon ceased, but the Inverness trips have gone from strength to strength. In 1988 the former Tyne ferry *Tyne Queen* was purchased and rebuilt, being renamed *Jacobite Queen*. 1988 saw the former Dutch vessel *Neptune's Lady* operate out of Banavie. She moved to Fort Augustus in 1989 but did not last long there. Various small vessels have operated out of Fort Augustus on Loch Ness cruises over the past twenty years or so.

Forth and Clyde Canal

This was the location of early steam vessel experiments with Symington's *Experiment* of 1789 and *Charlotte Dundas* of 1803. The horse-drawn boat *Cyclops* was converted to steam in 1830, followed by *Lord Dundas* in 1831 and *Manchester* in 1832. These had a paddle wheel in an inset in the hull aft and ran from Port Dundas to Lock 16 at Falkirk and on to Alloa and Stirling. These were all replaced in the early 1840s by horse-drawn Swift boats, which had the canal as their sole preserve until 1859, when *Rockvilla Castle* was built. From 1875 she ran for George Aitken from Port Dundas to Craigmarloch and Castlecary. He fell overboard and was drowned in 1880, and *Rockvilla Castle* was broken up after the 1881 season.

George Aitken's son, James, built the first *Fairy Queen* in 1893. She was sold in 1897 and replaced by a second steamer of the same name, which was joined by *May Queen* in 1903 and *Gipsy Queen* in 1905. *Fairy Queen* (II) was sold in 1921 and *May Queen* in 1918. A third *Fairy Queen*, a motor vessel, entered service in 1923, but was sold in 1931. *Gipsy Queen* remained in service until 1939. A competitor had appeared for a season in 1904 in the shape of steamer *Truro Belle*.

A revival of interest in canals led the Forth and Clyde Society to introduce a service with *Ferry Queen*, the former Clyde passenger ferry *Ferry No. 8,* in 1982 from the Stables Inn near Kirkintilloch. At the same time another ferry, *Ferry No. 10*, came into service there as a restaurant boat, much altered, and named *Caledonian*. In 1987 the restaurant boat *The Lady Margaret* entered service. The Seagull trust introduced cruises for the disabled with *Govan Seagull* and *Yarrow Seagull* in the late 1980s. The Forth and Clyde Canal Society introduced *Gipsy Princess* in 1990.

Union Canal

As far as is known, there were no engine-powered passenger vessels on the Union Canal before modern times. The Linlithgow Union Canal Society operates the steam outline passenger motor vessel *Victoria* and the excursion boat *Saint Magdalene* from Linlithgow. Ronnie Rusack of the Bridge Inn at Ratho operates the restaurant cruise vessels *Pride of the Union* and *Pride of Belhaven* from there, along with *Ratho Princess*, which formerly operated on the Norfolk Broads. The Seagull trust also operates *St John Crusader* and *Jane Telford* from there.

Other Lochs

Loch Arkaig

The Rifle was a small launch on this loch from the 1860s until 1939. She sank whilst being broken up in 1939. Her remains were raised from the loch bed in 1990 and are now at the Scottish Maritime Museum in Irvine.

Loch Earn

The motor vessel *Queen of Loch Earn* ran from 1922 to 1936 on Loch Earn.

Loch Eck

David Napier introduced a service on Loch Eck in 1820 with *Aglaia*, the first iron passenger vessel in the world. This was part of a through service from Glasgow to Inveraray. She lasted until around 1828. In 1878 a small screw steamer named *Fairy Queen* was built for the Glasgow and Inveraray Steamboat Company Ltd, and this offered part of a circular tour with *Lord of the Isles*. She was withdrawn during the First World War and scrapped in 1926.

Loch Maree

Mabel was operated on Loch Maree from 1883 until 1911, and was owned by David MacBrayne from 1887.

Loch Ossian

The steamer *Cailleach* operated on this loch from 1902 until the early 1930s, carrying guests and supplies to a shooting-lodge.

Loch Rannoch

The steamer *Gitana* was built in 1881 for this loch but sank at her moorings in February 1882. She was raised from the bed of the loch in the 1970s but never re-entered service. She was driven ashore in a storm and wrecked in 1983, when restoration was almost complete.

Loch Treig

The puffer *Loch Treig* ran here in connection with the construction of the West Highland Railway in 1894.

Loch Ericht, Loch Morar, Lake of Menteith, Lanark Loch

Small steam launches and motor vessels also ran on these lochs.

Acknowledgements

My thanks go to: Iain Quinn; Geoffrey Hamer; J.D. Stevenson, Edinburgh; the staff of the Mitchell Library, Glasgow, for access to the Langmuir Collection; and the Clyde River Steamer Club for the use of postcards produced by them and images from magazines and booklets published by them.

one

Loch Lomond, the Railway Steamers

Above: Marion was the first steamer to operate on Loch Lomond, entering service in the summer of 1818 for David Napier. She had been built the previous year by A. MacLachlan of Dumbarton with side-lever machinery by David Napier, and had operated in that summer from Glasgow to Greenock. In November 1817 she sailed up the river as far as the Clyde Ironworks at Dalmarnock,

which is the furthest any steamer has ever sailed up the Clyde. At that time the Leven was navigable, as the weirs were not built. The journey up the Leven was tricky, and was never made by any steamer in regular service, as far as is known. She was moved to Loch Lomond and commenced sailing there in 1818, as can be seen in this newspaper advertisement for the following year. Rob Roy's cave was around ¾ mile north of Inversnaid, and had no known association with the outlaw. The name was given to it by Napier in an early application of spin. (G.E. Langmuir Collection, Mitchell Library, Glasgow)

Right: An advertisement for *Marion*, showing a connection from Glasgow to Dumbarton, with connecting carriages to Balloch, by 'the Dumbarton Steam Boat'. *Dumbarton* was built in 1820 for a service from Glasgow to Dumbarton. *Marion* continued on the loch until she was replaced by *Euphrosyne* in 1827, and was then sold. She ran aground on her way down the Leven but was salvaged and later ran as a ferry across Loch Fyne until around 1832. (G.E. Langmuir Collection, Mitchell Library, Glasgow)

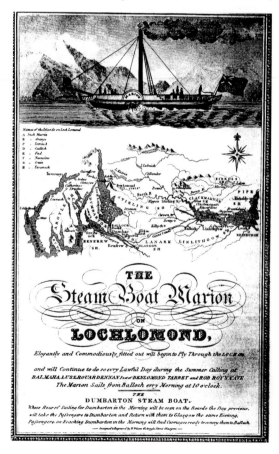

In 1825, competition came to the loch. A new steamer, named *Lady of the Lake*, was built for the Lochlomond Steamboat Co. Ltd. In 1827, David Napier moved *Post Boy*, which had been built in 1820 by William Denny of Dumbarton. Denny had taken over the yard of MacLachlan in 1818 for his service from Glasgow to Dumbarton and Gourock to Loch Lomond. *Post Boy* was replaced and renamed *Euphrosyne*. She was sold off the loch in 1838.

The Lochlomond Steamboat Co. got into financial difficulties in 1828 and was replaced by another company of the same name. In 1829 David Napier joined forces with John McMurrich, who was one of the partners in the Lochlomond Steamboat Co., and the firm of Napier and McMurrich thenceforth owned the loch steamers. *Lady of the Lake* was broken up in 1834. (G.E. Langmuir Collection, Mitchell Library, Glasgow)

Balloch, which had been built by John Wood of Port Glasgow, entered service in the following year. She was sold off the loch after only about one year, to the Dumbarton Steamboat Co., and became their *Dumbuck* (some sources state that she was built as *Robert Napier*, but John Wood built the steamer of that name in 1832 for service out of Londonderry). She is seen here as *Dumbuck*.

A new steamer named *Lochlomond*, which was the first iron steamer on the loch, entered service in 1836. She was sold off the loch in 1846 for service on the Caledonian Canal.

Another competitor arrived in 1838 in the shape of *Queen of Scots*, which had previously operated on the Clyde from Glasgow to Arrochar. It was operated by Lewis McLellan, who had been a partner in the former Lochlomond Steamboat Co. She continued on the loch until the 1841 season only. (Wotherspoon Collection, Mitchell Library, Glasgow)

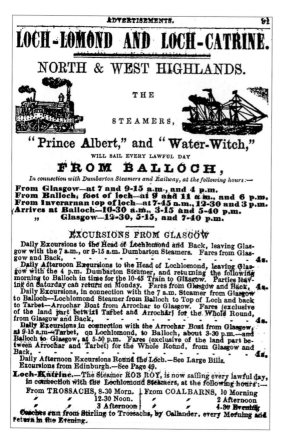

Waterwitch had been launched on 2 August 1843 by Caird's of Greenock for the Glasgow and Kilmun Steam Packet Co., and was purchased in April 1844 by John Bell of Dumbarton for a new service on Loch Lomond. The New Loch Lomond Steamboat Company was formed to operate her on a year-round service from Balloch to Inverarnan, up the River Falloch from Ardlui. Connecting coaches for Inverness and Killin ran from Inverarnan. Inversnaid had replaced Rob Roy's cave as a call in 1827 and by this time a coach connection was made from Inversnaid to Loch Catrine, as Loch Katrine was known in the parlance of the time.

Fierce competition between the new company and Napier and McMurrich lasted through the summer of 1844, but in April 1845 the two companies merged, and the new company became known as the Lochlomond Steamboat Company.

In 1847 a steamer named *Marchioness of Breadalbane* was ordered for the loch service from William Denny, but she did not conform to specifications and was not accepted by the company.

Prince Albert was built in 1850 and introduced the royal names which lasted until the introduction of *Maid of the Loch* 103 years later. Prince Albert himself had sailed on *Waterwitch* in 1849. Wm. Denny & Co. built *Prince Albert* with two-cylinder diagonal machinery by Caird's. She remained on the loch until she was sold in 1862. She then spent one season on the Clyde, probably on the Arrochar service, before being sold for service as a Mersey ferry. She was renamed *Richmond*, and ran from Liverpool to Eastham until 1872.

On 15 July 1850 the Caledonian and Dumbartonshire Junction Railway was opened from Bowling and Dumbarton to Balloch, and a through railway route was in operation to Glasgow from 1858. This company became part of the Edinburgh and Glasgow Railway in 1862, with the latter becoming part of the North British Railway in 1865.

In 1850, G. & J. Burns purchased David Napier's share of the Lochlomond Steamboat Co. and placed *Pilot* on the loch. She had been one of a trio of steamers built for the Glasgow and Greenock Railway's Railway Steamboat Company in 1844. On 19 July 1850 she ran aground on a rock off Rowardennan, which has since been known as the Pilot Rock. She was raised and continued to ply on the loch for the remainder of that season.

In the winter of 1851–52, *Waterwitch* was scrapped because her hull was corroded. Her machinery was placed in a new steamer from Alex Denny & Bros, which was named *Queen Victoria*. The latter was sold in 1868 to an owner at Whitby. She was renamed *Swallow*, and ran trips on the Wash until she was sold for service as a Mersey ferry from Liverpool to Seacombe in 1877. She was scrapped in 1883.

The above undated advertisement must therefore have been for the 1850 or 1851 season. (G.E. Langmuir Collection, Mitchell Library, Glasgow)

In 1857, *Prince of Wales* was ordered from Scott Sinclair of Greenock, who sub-contracted Laurence Hill & Co. to build the hull. She did not arrive on the loch until 1858, and entered service in the July of that year. On 12 September 1860 she ran aground on a submerged rock north-east of Inchmurrin, but was refloated and towed to Balloch. She had to be towed to a yard at Bowling for repairs. She was fitted with deck saloons in 1864 and had a long life on the loch, being sold for use as a coal hulk at Newry in 1901. She is seen here leaving Tarbet *c.* 1898. (From *Clyde Steamers* magazine)

The winter of 1894–95 was very cold and the Loch Lomond steamers were frozen in from the end of January to late February. *The Queen* was used as a restaurant at that time and *Prince of Wales* is seen here frozen in at Balloch pier. *Prince of Wales* was withdrawn in July 1899, by which time she was worn out. (From *Clyde Steamers* magazine)

Prince Consort was built in 1862 by Caird & Co. to replace *Prince Albert*, and was the first Loch Lomond steamer to have full-length sponsons rather than just around the paddle wheel. She is seen here approaching Luss, with Ben Lomond in the background, in the North British funnel colours between 1882 and 1896.

Prince Consort at Ardlui pier. Sailings up the River Falloch to Inverarnan ceased in around 1868. The pattern of calls at Balmaha, Luss, Rowardennan, Tarbet, Inversnaid and Ardlui was established, which, with the exception of the closure of certain piers, was to last until the withdrawal of *Countess Fiona* in 1989. *Prince Consort* was sold in December 1898 for breaking up on the arrival of *Princess May* and *Prince George*.

Princess of Wales was built in 1866 by Aitken and Mansell, and replaced *Queen Victoria*. She did not last on the loch for as long as her predecessor, and had no fore-saloon. She was sold to M. Brydie of Alloa in October 1881 for the service from Leith to Stirling. The owner died in 1885, and his executor moved her to the Tay to sail between Perth and Dundee, which she did until 1887. She saw further service on the Tay in 1891 as *Albion*. She spent 1901 to 1903 at Newcastle but returned to the Tay as *Shamrock* in 1904, which can be seen above. By this time her aft-saloon had been cut back almost to the level of the paddle boxes. In 1909 she was sold to London owners and later went to France, with her registry being closed in 1912. (G.E. Langmuir Collection, Mitchell Library, Glasgow)

The Queen was built in late 1883 by Caird & Co of Greenock to replace *Prince of Wales*. She had conventional sponsons and still had alleyways round the fore and aft saloons. (From *Clyde Steamers* magazine)

The *Queen* on the slipway at Balloch. This slipway was built in 1902 and is still in existence. It is currently the subject of a lottery grant, which is for the repair of the trolley and the restoration of the slipway, so that the slipway can be used in the preservation of *Maid of the Loch*.

A side-on view of *The Queen* on the slipway. She ran aground on a sandbank off Rossdhu Point on 15 June 1896, and could not be freed until 10 July, after rain had raised the level of the loch. In 1911 she was replaced by *Prince Edward* and was sold for breaking up in the April of that year. (From *Clyde Steamers* magazine)

TARBET, LOCH LOMOND

Empress was a sister of *The Queen* and came in 1888 from Napier, Shanks and Bell with machinery by D. Rowan. She is seen here in Balloch Bay in a postcard view in NB colours at Tarbet. While she was fitting out in December 1888, the Loch Lomond Steamboat Company sold out to the North British Steam Packet Company, which was owned by the North British Railway. She ran trials in the Gareloch on 18 December 1888, but it was January 1890 before she reached Loch Lomond.

In October 1896, the Dumbarton to Balloch railway and the Loch Lomond steamers were taken over the Dumbarton and Balloch Joint Line Committee, which was jointly owned by the North British and Caledonian Railways. The steamers changed their funnel colours to red with a black top, and this was the colour scheme in use when this photograph of a smoky *Empress* leaving Luss was taken.

Empress was re-boilered in 1915 and is seen at full speed in Balloch Bay in the 1920-25 era. (PSPS collection, courtesy of Robin Boyd)

Empress was laid up after the 1925 summer season in Drumkinnon Bay, as seen in this postcard view. She was eventually sold for breaking up in 1933.

By 1897, *Prince Consort* and *Prince of Wales* were worn out and in need of replacement. The two partners in the joint committee failed to reach agreement on the size of the steamers and the type of machinery to be built. Two steamers were eventually ordered from A. & J. Inglis and *Princess May* was launched on 11 October 1898, followed by *Prince George* six days later. Both had simple expansion diagonal machinery like their predecessors. *Princess May* ran trials on the Gareloch prior to being taken up the Leven to Loch Lomond, partly under her own power and partly being dragged by a dozen draught horses. She reached the loch on 8 November and Prince George on 6 December. Both entered service in May 1899. For the first time on a Loch Lomond steamer with normal sponson design, the deck saloons were the full width of the hull. In this picture *Prince George* is in mid-loch.

Prince George approaching Tarbet.

Prince George or *Princess May* arriving at Luss pier in a Judge's postcard view.

A postcard showing *Prince George* from the stern at Ardlui. She was a spare and a stand-by steamer from 1936 onwards. She was requisitioned by the Admiralty for a brief period in 1942 as an accommodation ship for tank pumping station employees evacuated from their homes following the Clydebank blitz. She was sold for scrapping later that year.

THE PIER, BALLOCH, SHOWING BEN LOMOND IN DISTANCE.   A.454.

This postcard view shows *Princess May* to the left, at the slipway jetty, with *Prince Edward* to the right at Balloch pier. It was posted with Edward VIII stamps, but the postmark is obscured. The message reads: 'Had a cruise on *Princess Patricia* for 9d'.

99295 JV   BALMAHA, LOCH LOMOND.

Princess May or *Prince George* leaving Balmaha pier in another postcard view. This was posted in 1934.

Princess May at Tarbert in a pre–1914 'tartan' postcard.

A large crowd of passengers boarding *Princess May* in another 'tartan' postcard dated 1917. They are presumably from the Loch Katrine coaches at Inversnaid.

Princess May and *Prince George* are berthed at Ardlui pier.

A lightly filled *Princess May* arriving at Tarbet.

Princess May with an LMS/LNER house flag flying after 1923. She is passing Balloch Castle.

Princess May at Balloch in the early season of 1948, with a black-topped yellow funnel. From 1925 onwards a Sunday service was given on the loch, and in December 1932 the winter service was dropped. From 1933 to 1935 *Princess May* was a spare vessel, but from 1936 onwards she returned to the main sailings. At some time in the 1930s, *Princess May* lost her mast, probably due to Loch Lomond wood rot, and continued sailing without it.

This is *Princess May* at the slipway pier at Balloch later in 1948. She has a white line with a black line above it, along the waterline. (G.E. Langmuir Collection, Mitchell Library, Glasgow)

In May 1949, *Princess May* and *Prince Edward*, now under British Railways ownership, received a black hull. This is visible in this shot of *Princess May* arriving at Tarbet in that summer. She was broken up at Balloch in the June and July of 1953, following the arrival of *Maid of the Loch*. (Douglas McGowan collection)

In 1911 the final pre-1914 steamer to be constructed for the Loch Lomond service, *Prince Edward*, was built at the A. & J. Inglis yard at Pointhouse, at the mouth of the Kelvin. She was 10ft longer than *Prince George* and *Princess May* and differed from them in having compound machinery. She left the Kelvin on 4 May and was steamed down the Clyde and up the Leven to Kirkland, leaving Pointhouse on 4 May and taking five days to proceed that far up the Leven with the help of two horses, which were pulled into the river, and teams of men pulling her. To get her under the bridge at Bonhill, volunteer members of the public and, according to legend, classes of local schoolchildren were called on to weigh her down to get her under the bridge. She spent the summer at Kirkland, finally reaching Loch Lomond on 6 November. (From *Clyde Steamers* magazine)

Prince Edward entered service on the loch on 1 June 1912, effectively replacing *The Queen*, which had been scrapped in the previous year. She is seen here arriving at Tarbet.

Right: The August and September 1914 timetable for Loch Lomond shows both the Caledonian Railway connections from Glasgow central low level and the North British ones from Glasgow Queen Street low level. (From *Clyde Steamers* magazine)

Below: Prince Edward on the slipway at Balloch.

CALEDONIAN and NORTH BRITISH RAILWAYS

LOCH-LOMOND STEAMERS

SERVICE for SEPTEMBER, 1914, and until further notice

TRAIN.		a.m.	a.m.	p.m.	p.m.
GLASGOW (Central Low Level)	... dep.	9 26	—	—	4 2
GLASGOW (Queen Street Low Level)	"	—	9 †35	4 0	—
BALLOCH PIER	... arr.	10 26	10 26	4 42	4 48

STEAMER.				
BALLOCH PIER	... dep.	10 35		4 50
BALMAHA	"	11 5		5 15
LUSS	"	11 25		5 35
ROWARDENNAN	"	11 45		5 50
TARBET	"	12 5		6 10
INVERSNAID	"	12 25		6 25
ARDLUI	... arr.	12 45		6 50

Daily in September. Thurs. and Sats. only from October to March inclusive.

Saturdays only and during September only.

† Change at Dumbarton.

STEAMER.		a.m.	p.m.	p.m.
ARDLUI	... dep.	6 30	2 30	4 10
INVERSNAID	"	6 55	2 55	4 35
TARBET	"	7 10	3 10	4 55
ROWARDENNAN	"	7 30	3 30	5 15
LUSS	"	7 50	3 50	5 33
BALMAHA	"	8 5	4 10	5 50
BALLOCH PIER	... arr.	8 35	4 40	6 20

Mondays only and during September only.

Sats. only in September. Tues., Thurs., and Sats. only from October to March inclusive.

Daily except Sats. and during September only.

TRAIN.		a.m.	a.m.	p.m.	p.m.
BALLOCH PIER	... dep.	8 40	8 40	4845	6 25
GLASGOW (Central Low Level)	... arr.	9 33	—	—	—
GLASGOW (Queen Street Low Level)	"	—	9 30	5/50	7 17

b 4.50 p.m. on Saturdays.   f 5.54 p.m. on Saturdays.

DONALD A. MATHESON,
General Manager,
Caledonian Railway.

W. F. JACKSON,
General Manager,
North British Railway.

GLASGOW, August, 1914.   MCCORQUODALE & CO. LTD., GLASGOW & LONDON.

S. S. 'Prince' Edward at Balloch.

Prince Edward arriving at Balloch pier.

Luss Village, Loch Lomond

369

Prince Edward at Luss.

A postcard view shows *Prince Edward* arriving at Tarbet pier.

Like the other Loch Lomond steamers, by the mid-1930s *Prince Edward* had lost her mast. She is seen here north of Luss. (G. Grimshaw)

Like *Princess May*, *Prince Edward*, seen here at Balloch, received a yellow funnel in 1948 and a black hull in 1949 following nationalisation. (Douglas McGowan collection)

Prince Edward continued in service over the 1953 and 1954 summers, alongside *Maid of the Loch*. At this time she had a white hull and paddle-boxes. At the beginning of the 1953 season her funnel was painted all yellow, which was how it was when this photograph was taken of her leaving Ardlui. (G.E. Langmuir Collection, Mitchell Library, Glasgow)

After a few weeks, before the end of May 1953, a half-height black top was added because the coal smoke was darkening the all-yellow top to the funnel. She is seen here leaving Ardlui. (G.E. Langmuir Collection, Mitchell Library, Glasgow)

By August 1953 the full black top was reinstated. *Prince Edward*, seen here leaving Ardlui, was withdrawn at the end of the 1954 season, and was broken up on the slipway at Balloch in April 1955.

The L. C. C. New River Boat "Vanbrugh."

In 1914, two of the fleet of paddle steamers built in 1905 for London County Council, *Shakespeare* and *Earl Godwin*, were purchased for Loch Lomond. They were built by Thornycroft and by Napier and Miller respectively, both with compound machinery by Scott's of Greenock. London County Council withdrew their service on economic grounds in 1907, and these two were amongst ten steamers which were sold at that time to the City Steam-Boat Co. This postcard depicts *Vanbrugh*, but is a standard postcard used for all the LCC steamers.

Shakespeare was renamed *Princess Patricia* and *Earl Godwin* was renamed *Queen Mary*. *Queen Mary* was damaged by fire shortly after arriving at Loch Lomond and never saw service. She was sold for scrapping in 1928 and no close-up photographs of her are known to survive. *Princess Patricia* was intended for winter service, but she saw little of that and was mainly employed on short cruises out of Balloch.

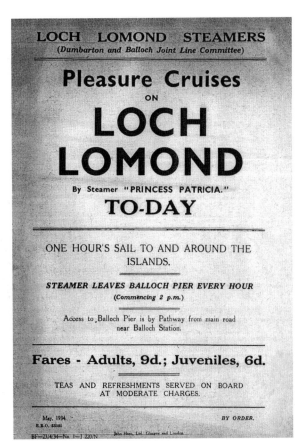

Right: A 1934 advertisement for cruises from Balloch by *Princess Patricia*. She was used during 1936 in the shooting of the film *Spy of Napoleon*, and was disguised as a Lake Geneva paddle steamer. She was withdrawn after the 1938 season, and was sold for breaking up on the slipway at Balloch.

The railway nationalisation of 1948 saw the end of the Dumbarton and Balloch Joint Committee. The ownership of the Loch Lomond steamers passed to the Scottish Region of British Railways. Luss pier, whish was in poor condition, closed at the end of the 1951 season. In 1950, as part of the modernisation programme for the Caledonian Steam Packet Co., an order was placed with A. & J. Inglis for a new paddle steamer for the loch. *Maid of the Loch* was initially erected at Inglis' Pointhouse yard, and was then transferred in sections to Balloch to be re-erected, which is shown in this picture. Note *Princess May* astern of the *Maid*. It is alleged that *Maid of the Loch*'s name was originally to be *Princess Anne*. (G.E. Langmuir Collection, Mitchell Library, Glasgow)

Maid of the Loch was re-erected at Balloch in 1952. She was considerably larger then her predecessors and was engined by Rankin and Blackmore of Greenock. Her hull was a variation on that of the CSP steamer *Marchioness of Lorne* of 1935, although she had conventional paddle boxes with the traditional Loch Lomond horizontal slatted vents rather than the disguised paddle boxes of the Clyde counterpart, companionways in the sponsons (typical for Loch Lomond paddle steamers) and a cafeteria aft on the main deck with windows right round the stern. Her compound diagonal engines were supposedly an improved version of those built for *Kylemore* in 1897. She was thus rather an anachronism, although one concession to modernity was the fact that her superstructure was made of aluminium. The funnel originally had a black top, but was entirely painted yellow by the time she entered service. (G.E. Langmuir Collection, Mitchell Library, Glasgow)

Left: Maid of the Loch at Balloch pier.

Below: Maid of the Loch had a relatively uneventful life on the loch. She is seen here at Ardlui pier, which was closed at the end of the 1963 season. A cruise to the head of the loch replaced the call there on certain sailings, and others only went as far as Inversnaid. (Loch Lomond Steamships Company)

TRAIN AND STEAMER SERVICES TO AND FROM LOCH LOMOND
23rd MAY until 11th SEPTEMBER, 1955

OUTWARD

OUTWARD	MONDAYS to FRIDAYS	TUESDAYS and THURSDAYS ONLY	SATURDAYS (a.m.)	SATURDAYS (a.m. — Commences 2nd July)	SATURDAYS (p.m. — Commences 25th June)	SUNDAYS
TRAIN	a.m.	p.m.	a.m.	a.m.	p.m.	a.m.
EDINBURGH (Waverley) ... leave	9 5	1 0	8 10	9 5	1 0	11 0
GLASGOW (Queen Street Low Level) ... "	10 23	2 55	9 25	10 23	2 15	1 18p.m.
PARTICK HILL ... "	10 32	3 4	9 34	10 32	2 24	1 26
ANNIESLAND ... "	10 37	3 9	9 39	10 37	2 29	1 31
DRUMCHAPEL ... "	10 42	3 14	9 44	10 42	2 34	1 38
SINGER ... "	10 48	3 18	9 50	10 48	2 38	1 44
DUMBARTON (Central) ... "	11 2	3 29	10 3	11 2	2 49	1 45
ALEXANDRIA and BONHILL ... "	11 8	3 35	10 10	11 8	2 55	1 51
BALLOCH (Central) ... "	11 17	3 43	10 18	11 17	3 3	2 10
BALLOCH PIER ... arrive	11 19	3 45	10 20	11 19	3 5	2 12
STEAMER						
BALLOCH PIER ... leave	11 25	4 0	10 30	11 25	3 15	2 30
BALMAHA ... arrive	11 55	—	11 0	11 55	3 45	3 0
ROWARDENNAN (For Ben Lomond) ... "	12 35p.m.	—	11 40	12 35p.m.	4 25	3 40
TARBET (For Loch Long) ... "	1 0	—	12 20	1 0	4 30	4 5
INVERSNAID (For Trossachs) ... "	1 15	5 15	12 50	1 15	5 5	4 20
ARDLUI (Head of Loch) ... "	1 45	5 45	—	1 45	5 35	4 50

(TUESDAYS and THURSDAYS ONLY column: Commences on 31st May and does not run on Thursday 7th July)

RETURN

RETURN	MONDAYS WEDNESDAYS and FRIDAYS	TUESDAYS and THURSDAYS (Commences on 31st May)	TUESDAYS and THURSDAYS (24th and 26th May only)	SATURDAYS	SATURDAYS (Commences 2nd July)	SATURDAYS	SUNDAYS
STEAMER	p.m.	p.m.	p.m.	p.m.	p.m.	p.m.	p.m.
ARDLUI ... leave	4 15	1 50	4 15	6 30	1 0	4 15	6 0
INVERSNAID ... "	4 45	2 20	4 45	7 0	1 30	4 45	6 30
TARBET ... "	5 0	2 40	5 0	7 15	1 45	5 0	6 45
ROWARDENNAN ... "	5 25	—	5 25	7 40	—	5 25	7 10
BALMAHA ... "	6 5	—	6 5	8 20	—	6 5	7 50
BALLOCH PIER ... arrive	6 30	3 55	6 30	8 45	3 0	6 30	8 15
TRAIN							
BALLOCH PIER ... leave	6 40	4 20	6 40	8 55	3 10	6 40	8 30
BALLOCH (Central) ... arrive	6 42	4 22	6 42	8 57	3 12	6 42	8 32
ALEXANDRIA and BONHILL ... "	6 52	4 30	6 52	9 5	3 19	6 52	8 40
DUMBARTON (Central) ... "	7d13	4 42	7d13	9 14	3 30	7d13	8 45
SINGER ... "	—	5c21	—	9 28	3 43	—	8 57
DRUMCHAPEL ... "	—	—	—	9 33	3 49	—	9 3
ANNIESLAND ... "	7 23	—	7 23	9 39	3 56	7 23	9 12
PARTICK HILL ... "	7 31	5e26	7 31	9 43	4 0	7 31	9 16
GLASGOW (Queen Street Low Level) ... "				9 51	4 8		9 24
EDINBURGH (Waverley) ... "	9 16	7 16	9 16	11 15	6 10	9 16	10f53

(SATURDAYS return: run on Thursday 7th July)

c Arrives Partick (Central) Station   d Arrives Clydebank (Central) Station   e Arrives Glasgow (Central Low Level) Station   f Commences 19th June

Full particulars of connecting train services from other stations can be obtained at Railway Booking and Enquiry Offices.

The 1955 Loch Lomond timetable. By this time the train connections were almost all from Glasgow Queen Street low level. The central low level line had started the decline that led to its closure in 1964.

The cover of the 1955 summer Loch Lomond steamer timetable, with a painting of *Maid of the Loch*, travelling at speed. This cover was used each summer from 1953 to 1959.

ATTRACTIVE DAY TOURS

FROM GLASGOW

embracing

LOCH LOMOND,

LOCH LOMOND — LOCH KATRINE TROSSACHS and CALLANDER

TOUR No. 1

DAILY (Mondays to Saturdays, 23rd May until 10th September)

Leaving Glasgow (Queen Street Low Level) at 10.23 a.m. Mondays to Fridays; 10.23 a.m. Saturdays until 25th June; and 9.25 a.m. Saturdays commencing 2nd July for Balloch Pier, thence by Steamer on Loch Lomond to Inversnaid. Motor from Inversnaid to Stronachlachar and Steamer on Loch Katrine from Stronachlachar to Trossachs Pier, thence by motor to Callander and home from Callander by rail, arriving Glasgow (Buchanan St.) at 7.11 p.m. The Tour can also be made in the reverse direction.

1st Class Rail		TOUR FARES	3rd Class Rail	
Adults	Juveniles	from	Adults	Juveniles
24/9	13/-	GLASGOW	21/3	11/3

THREE LOCHS — LOCH LOMOND, LOCH LONG and LOCH GOIL

TOUR No. 5—28th May until 10th September

TUESDAYS, and THURSDAYS

Leaving Glasgow (Queen Street Low Level) at 10.23 a.m. for Balloch Pier, thence by Steamer on Loch Lomond to Tarbet Pier. Passengers then find their own way from Tarbet Pier to Arrochar Pier and board Steamer for sail down Loch Long via Loch Goil to Gourock and Craigendoran, arriving back Glasgow (Central) at 4.55 p.m. (via Gourock) and Glasgow (Queen Street) at 5.23 p.m. (via Craigendoran)

The Tour can also be made in the reverse direction leaving Glasgow (Queen Street Low Level) at 9.10 a.m. (via Craigendoran) or Glasgow (Central) at 9.30 a.m. (via Gourock), arriving back at Glasgow (Queen Street) at 5.23 p.m.

SATURDAYS

Leaving Glasgow (Queen Street) at 10.23 a.m. 28th May until 25th June; and 9.25 a.m. 2nd July until 10th September for Balloch Pier, thence by steamer on Loch Lomond to Tarbet Pier. Passengers then find their own way from Tarbet Pier to Arrochar Pier and board steamer for sail down Loch Long via Loch Goil to Gourock and Craigendoran, arriving back at Glasgow (Central) at 8.26 p.m. (via Gourock) and Glasgow (Queen Street) at 8.53 p.m. (via Craigendoran)

The Tour can also be made in the reverse direction leaving Glasgow (Queen Street Low Level) at 10.38 a.m. (via Craigendoran) or Glasgow (Central) at 11.10 a.m. (via Gourock), arriving back at Glasgow (Queen Street) at 7.31 p.m. 28th May until 25th June; and 9.48 p.m. 2nd July until 10th September.

1st Class Rail	TOUR FARES	3rd Class Rail
14/3	from GLASGOW	12/6

The tickets are valid on the date for which issued

The Loch Lomond steamer service could be used as part of two circular tours; the Three Loch tour and the Loch Katrine tour.

Maid of the Loch approaching Rowardennan. This was, of all the piers, the trickiest to come alongside.

Rowardennan pier was rebuilt in 1978. It was always busy with those who went to climb Ben Lomond.

Maid of the Loch, with a damaged fore-saloon window, at Tarbet in a postcard view.

Maid of the Loch at Inversnaid in the early 1970s.

Maid of the Loch at Inversnaid with the Inversnaid Hotel's passenger launch in the foreground.

Maid of the Loch in mid-loch in the mid to late 1960s.

Above left: Reflections: *Maid of the Loch* laid up at Balloch in winter.

Above right: Lost in the trees: *Maid of the Loch* glimpsed through the encroaching vegetation on the slipway at Balloch.

Above: Maid of the Loch on the slipway in the late 1970s.

Left: Maid of the Loch on the slipway trolley. The repair of this is to be the major part of the proposed overhaul of the slipway.

Above: The paddle box and crest of *Maid of the Loch*.

Right: The sponson and paddle box of *Maid of the Loch*, seen here while on the slipway.

Above: Detail of the paddles. She was fitted with wooden floats, rather than the more modern metal floats.

Left: The rudder of *Maid of the Loch* with Balloch pier in the background. This was an unbalanced (barn door type) rudder like that fitted on Waverley (1947). An additional welded piece was added at the base as seen here.

Right: The steam winding engine at the top of the slipway at Balloch.

Below: Another view of the steam winding engine.

The builder's plate of the winding engine, built by John Bennie of the Star Engine Works, Glasgow.

The boiler for the steam winding engine at Balloch, named *Fred*, was apparently a former steam locomotive boiler. It was removed shortly after this photograph was taken in early 1988.

The upper deck on *Maid of the Loch* on a choppy day.

On 11 June 1978, a plaque was unveiled on *Maid of the Loch* to mark her golden jubilee. Note Mr Whittle (at the left-hand side of the plaque) from Caledonian MacBrayne and Mrs Mona Moore and Mr James Moore (at the right-hand side) from the PSPS.

The aforementioned plaque, donated by the Paddle Steamer Preservation Society (Scottish branch). This was unveiled by Mrs Mona Moore and shows the CalMac and PSPS (Scottish branch) flags.

The engines of *Maid of the Loch*.

In January 1957, the ownership of *Maid of the Loch* passed to the Caledonian Steam Packet Co. Ltd. On 1 January 1969 the CSP became part of the Scottish Transport Group. In the summer of that year, the ownership of *Maid of the Loch* was transferred to the bus operator Walter Alexander & Sons (Midland) Ltd, although she was still operated by the CSP. 1973 saw the formation of Caledonian MacBrayne Ltd, but thankfully, *Maid of the Loch* was spared their funnel colours.

In 1975, *Maid of the Loch* started the season with a black top to her yellow funnel.

From 4 June 1975, her funnel was painted red with a narrower black top, but reverted to all-over yellow for the summer of 1976. For a brief period she ran with a yellow band between the red and black portions.

Left: Maid of the Loch survived in service to celebrate her silver jubilee in 1978. This was marked by the issue of a special postcard by Caledonian MacBrayne.

Below: The 1978 timetable for *Maid of the Loch*. Balmaha pier had closed in 1971, and Tarbet pier in 1975, leaving only the Balloch, Rowardennan and Inversnaid piers open.

Paddle Steamer 'Maid of the Loch'

Sailings on Loch Lomond 27th May until 9th September 1978

		Monday to Friday			Saturday and Sunday	
			W		A	
Balloch Pier	depart	1040	1440	1940	1110	1440
Rowardennan	arrive	1140	1540	–	1210	1640
Inversnaid	arrive	1220	1620	–	–	–
Inversnaid	depart	1230	1630	–	–	–
Rowardennan	depart	1310	1710	–	1210	1640
Balloch Pier	arrive	1420	1820	2150	1350	1740

Code A - not on Saturday 24th June

    W - Wednesday only 'Showboat' ceases after
        16th August - on 9th and 16th August arrives
        back 30 minutes later.

Special Rates for Parties

Full Details from Caledonian MacBrayne Ltd., The Pier, Gourock, PA19 1QP

Caledonian MacBrayne

walkerprint
London 01 636 8560

In spring 1978 *Maid of the Loch* lost her main mast, as her predecessors had lost theirs in the 1930s.

Luss pier was re-opened on 24 May 1980.

Maid of the Loch arriving at Luss on 24 May 1980.

Maid of the Loch departing from Luss on the same occasion.

By this time in her career, *Maid of the Loch* was suffering from boiler problems and would give out large bursts of black or white smoke.

1981 was the final operational season for *Maid of the Loch*. She is seen here leaving Luss in the June of that year. Her last day in service was 30 August 1981.

Maid of the Loch on the slipway in spring 1981, with scaffolding surrounding her funnel and a red paddle box. This paint was presumably the undercoat.

In 1981, as a last-gasp attempt at publicity, a bus painted with an illustration of *Maid of the Loch* was used as an advertising medium.

From 1982 onwards, *Maid of the Loch* lay at Balloch, where she was used as a landing platform for *Countess Fiona*, and her condition steadily deteriorated.

Left: This is the poor condition of the paddle box, viewed from *Countess Fiona* in 1985.

Below: After various changes of ownership and abortive plans for her return to service, *Maid of the Loch* was purchased by Dumbarton District Council for preservation in 1992. The Loch Lomond Steamship Company was formed in 1995 and took over the ownership. Volunteers started a major programme of restoration, and she was fully painted. She had a black hull and a black-topped red funnel, after a period with a black-topped yellow one. She is shown here in May 1997.

Above: Maid of the Loch at an open day in May 1997.

Right: The ravages of time had virtually destroyed her interior fittings. This is the aft lounge, which had been the cafeteria, at the May 1997 open day, with a display of model ships.

In 1997, new steel decks were laid and toilets were fitted. The dining saloon and cafeteria re-opened as a restaurant and café. The aft deck saloon, which had been the bar, was restored by the family of the late Douglas Mickel, of house builders MacTaggart and Mickel. It is now known as the Douglas Mickel Saloon. The forward deck saloon has reverted to its previous use as a souvenir shop.

In 2002, her paddle boxes were painted black and a gold line was painted along her hull for the Queen's golden jubilee and her own golden jubilee in 2003. There are plans for her to be slipped as the next stage of her restoration, if lottery funding is available for restoration of the slipway.

The boiler was removed in the early nineties, and the machinery has been gradually restored. New boilers would need to be fitted if she is to return to service.

In March 1982 Ind Coope Alloa Brewery purchased *Maid of the Loch,* and in the following month they purchased *Countess of Kempock.* The latter had been built in 1936 for the Caledonian Steam Packet Co. Ltd for service on Loch Awe (see page 88), and had been moved to the Clyde in 1952. In 1971 she had been sold to Ritchie of Gourock and renamed *Countess of Kempock.* Offshore Workboats had purchased her in 1979 and she ran for a couple of seasons from Ulva Ferry to Staffa and Iona, and in 1981 out of Oban. She was lifted out of the water by the large crane at Stobcross Quay, and cut into three sections horizontally (hull, superstructure, and bridge) and re-erected at Balloch. She had to cross the Erskine Bridge twice en route to avoid a low bridge. She entered service on the loch on 16 June 1982, named *Countess Fiona.* A thin funnel had been added. She is seen here berthed alongside *Maid of the Loch* at Balloch in 1982.

Countess Fiona at Inversnaid in 1985.

Countess Fiona at Inversnaid in 1985 on the occasion of a Clyde River Steamer Club charter, on which she also called at Balmaha, becoming the first steamer to call there since *Maid of the Loch* in 1971.

Countess Fiona facing south at Inversnaid in 1982.

Right: In 1985 the Ind Coope logo was fitted to the funnel. In 1986 Balloch pier station was closed. The trains now terminate at a new station to the south of the level crossing on the main road through Balloch.

Below: In spring 1988, *Countess Fiona* was remodelled. Her funnel was replaced by a fatter, motor ship-type one. The old one is shown here lying on the ground near the slipway. The thin white band had been added around 1986.

Countess Fiona's saloon was widened to the full width of the hull and the bridge wings were moved forward so that they were level with the wheelhouse. She is seen here arriving at Luss in July 1989. She started the season with a second mast, but this was quickly removed.

Countess Fiona at Luss in July 1989. The alterations are visible.

Countess Fiona departing from Luss on the same occasion. In April 1989, *Countess Fiona* and *Maid of the Loch* were taken over by the Sea Management Corporation of Australia in association with James Fisher of Barrow. They announced plans to bring a Tasmanian-built catamaran, to be named *Lady of the Loch*. This vessel did not appear and Sea Management Corporation went into liquidation on 2 May 1990. *Countess Fiona* did not sail again. In 1990 she was hauled onto the slipway. Her final sailing in 1989 had taken her to off Ardlui.

Countess Fiona remained laid up on the slipway at Balloch through various changes of ownership, until, after gradually getting more vandalised, she was broken up by a bulldozer in September 1999. She is seen here in May 1997 with some of her saloon windows boarded up.

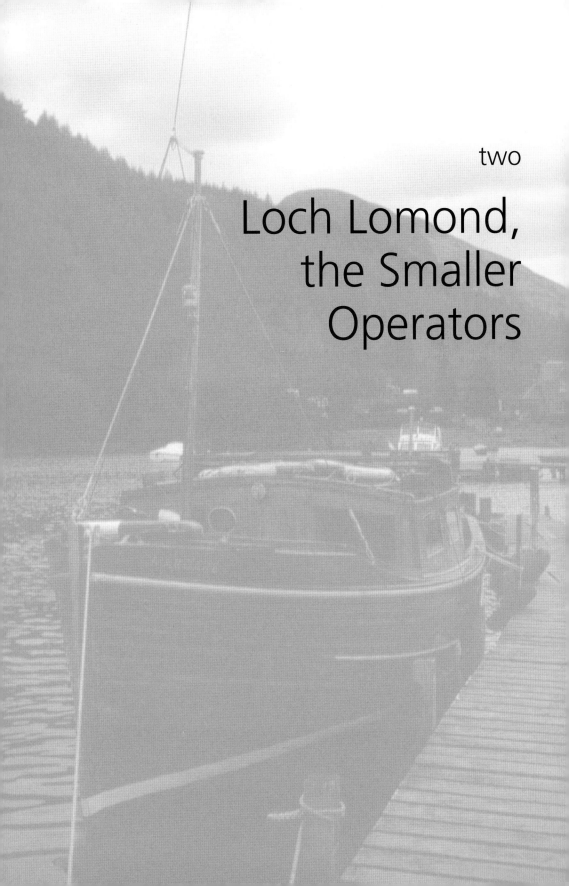

two

Loch Lomond, the Smaller Operators

From top:

From the early years of the twentieth century, short cruises and charters were offered by steam launches from Balloch, like the one seen on the left in this postcard view. They were operated by the firms of Lynn and Sweeney using a variety of vessels of which, as far as is known, there is no recorded history.

Powan was an early steam launch on Loch Lomond. She was still active on the loch in the early 1950s, and has survived, more recently sailing on Rutland Water. She is currently being restored at the Clyde Maritime Centre on the quayside near the sailing ship *Glenlee*.

The Sweeney family returned to owning boats in 1964 and operated 50-minute islands cruises from both Balloch Bridge and a new pontoon on the eastern side of the railway pier. They also ran afternoon cruises to Luss. Their most notable vessel is *Skylark IX*, which was built in 1928, and was present at Dunkirk. She is seen here at Luss in 2000. She was surplus following the merger of Sweeney and Mullen in 2002 and did not operate in the 2003 season.

The Leven at Balloch

Right: The Dunkirk plaque on *Skylark IX*. She was built by Bolson's of Poole to run trips from the beach at Bournemouth. During the war she served as a shallow water minesweeper in Poole harbour, and after the war was at Morecambe and Burntisland. In the fifties and early sixties she ran excursions from Portobello beach, before being purchased by Sweeney in around 1972.

Below: In 1992, Sweeney purchased the Thames excursion vessel *Silver Marlin*, which was built in 1966. With her covered accommodation and bar, she is ideal for the charter market.

Lomond Sunrise was built in 1942 and acquired by Sweeney in 1992. She is seen here on the slip at Balloch in spring 2003.

In 2002 Sweeney merged with the firm of Mullen, which was the successor to several firms operating from the east bank of the Leven at Balloch. This picture shows a line-up of excursion boats in the late 1970s, including *Lomond Duchess* and *Lomond Queen*. The former was built in 1974 as one of a pair for Loch Lomond Sailings, owned at that time by Nigel Stead, a director of the long vanished film processing company Gratispool. The latter was built in 1953 for the loch. Stead sold the company to the Mullen family around 1980.

Lomond Duchess at Balloch in Mullen livery in summer 2000.

Mullen also owned the Amsterdam-style waterbus, *Lomond Maid*.

A later *Lomond Maid* of Mullen, which was originally the Windermere launch *Belle Isle*, near Luss in 2000. She was sold to Wear Cruises of Sunderland and renamed *Brokaela* in 2001.

Lomond Monarch is the sister of the second *Lomond Maid*, and was built in 1971 as *Wynander* on Windermere. She remained in Mullen's fleet until the takeover by Sweeney, who renamed her *Glen Falloch*.

Above: Since 1948, the MacFarlane family have operated a post boat service from Balmaha to the inhabited Loch Lomond Islands. The boat used is *Marion*, which was built in 1939, and is pictured here.

Right: The larger *Margaret*, which was built in 1955, is also in MacFarlane's fleet.

The twelve-passenger *Lady Jean* is in the fleet as well.

Trips from Luss were popular in the late eighties and nineties because the television series *Take the High Road* was filmed there. This is *Glendarroch* in 1989, seen off Luss pier. *Glendarroch* was the fictional name of Luss village in the series.

An unidentified boat which was operating from the beach jetty at Luss in summer 2000.

Cruise Loch Lomond operates cruises from Tarbet where it is based, and from Inveruglas. Many of these are in connection with coach tours on their way north via the A82, which allows a break for the passengers and the driver. *Lomond Princess* was built in 1973 for Loch Lomond Sailings and is the sister of *Lomond Duchess*. The Tarbet operator acquired her in 1983.

Lomond Chieftain off Tarbet pier. She was built at Hull in 1972, and was previously in service on Loch Ness as *Jacobite Chieftain*. Cruise Loch Lomond purchased her in 1987. As can be seen here, the pier was rebuilt from its original form and would now be too low for calls by *Maid of the Loch* if and when she were to return to service. The original steamer pier was closed in 1975 and the rebuilt pier opened in 1984.

The first *Lomond Queen* lying at anchor off Tarbet in 1985. She was built in 1953 and was previously in the fleet of the Loch Lomond sailings at Balloch. She was sold in 1987 to Jacobite Cruises of Inverness, and became their *Jacobite Queen*. She is now named *Jacobite Warrior*.

The second *Lomond Queen*, which is the sister of *Lomond Chieftain*, off Tarbet in 1989. She was built in 1972 and was formerly *Jacobite Clansman* on Loch Ness. Then she became *Lochaber Lady* at Fort William for a short while, before being purchased by the Loch Lomond operator in 1988.

Lomond Mist, which was the former Amsterdam waterbus *Prinses Juliana*, at Tarbet in 1989. She was built in 1954 and was sold in 1998 for service on Derwentwater as *Lakeland Mist*.

Lomond Prince is the largest vessel operating for Cruise Loch Lomond out of Tarbet. She was built in 1978 and was acquired in 1996. She was formerly *Enchante* on the Thames in central London, and is seen here lying off Tarbet in August 2003.

The Inversnaid Hotel operates a boat for transferring guests who are on coach tours, from Inveruglas to the hotel. This is a former cruise ship tender, built in 1966 and named *Arklet*. She is seen here at the jetty at Inveruglas, along with *Lomond Princess*.

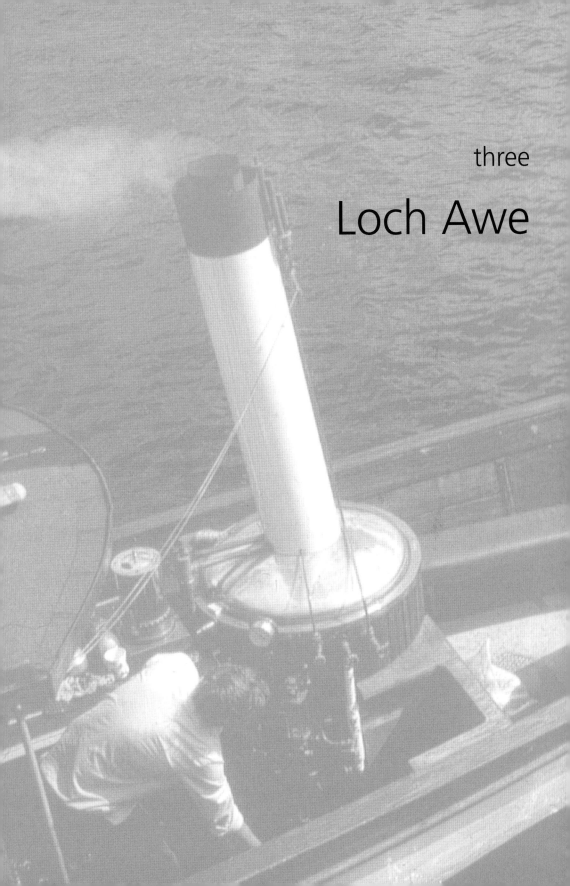

three

Loch Awe

Photographs of the first two steamers to ply on Loch Awe have not come to light. These were *Eva*, which ran in 1861 and 1862, and *Queen of the Lake* which was built in 1863 near Port Sonachan. *Queen of the Lake* was taken over by Hutcheson's in 1875 and ran for them until 1882.

Lochawe was built for Hutcheson's in 1876 by Muir and Caldwell, who sub-contacted the hull to A. & J. Inglis. She was erected at the lake, and had two-cylinder simple expansion machinery. *Lochawe* ran from Ford, at the southern end of the loch, and initially went to the Pass of Brander with a horse-coach connection to Oban and, from the opening of the Callander and Oban Railway in 1880, to Lochawe pier, adjacent to Lochawe station. Intermediate calls were made at New York, Port Sonachan and Cladich. (G.E. Langmuir Collection, Mitchell Library, Glasgow)

GLASGOW to OBAN via LOCHAWE.
CIRCULAR TOUR.

		TO OBAN *via Lochawe* RETURNING *via Crinan*					TO OBAN *via Crinan* RETURNING *via Lochawe*		
STEAMER		FROM	A.M.		STEAMER		FROM	A.M.	
		{ Glasgow.......at	7 0				{ Glasgow ....at	7 0	
			P.M.					P.M.	
COACH		(Ardrishaig...... ,,	12 40		'LINNET'		(Ardrishaig...... ,,	12 40	
STR.		{ Ardrishaig...... ,,	12 50				{ Ardrishaig...... ,,	1 0	
RAIL		{ Ford .... ,,	3 0				{ Crinan .... ,,	2 55	
		{ Ford .... ,,	3 0		STR.		{ Crinan .... ,,	3 0	
STR.		(Lochawe Pier.... ,,	5 20		RAIL		(Oban .... ,,	4 45	
'LINNET'		{ Lochawe Station ,,	5 36						A.M.
		(Oban .... ,,	6 25	A.M.	STR.		{ Oban .... ,,		8 0
		{ Oban .... ,,	8 0				(Lochawe Station ,,		8 50
		(Crinan .... ,,	10 0				{ Lochawe Pier ... ,,		9 0
					COACH		(Ford .... ,,		10 40
		{ Crinan .... ,,	10 0				{ Ford .... ,,		10 45
			P.M.		STR.				P.M.
		(Ardrishaig...... ,,	12 15				(Ardrishaig...... ,,		12 40
STR.		{ Ardrishaig...... ,,	1 0				{ Ardrishaig...... ,,		1 0
		(Glasgow........ ,,	6 45				(Glasgow .... ,,		6 45

MacBrayne's Loch Awe service, with a coach connection from Ardrishaig, offered an alternative to the Ardrishaig to Oban canal-and-sea section of the Royal Route. It was offered as a circular tour, which can be seen in this timetable from 1884.

Lochawe with *Countess of Breadalbane* at Ford pier. *Lochawe* became part of the MacBrayne fleet in 1879. She was laid up after the outbreak of war in August 1914 and scrapped in 1924.

The nearest steamer in this postcard view of Port Sonochan is *Kilchurn Castle*, which was built in 1883 for the owner of the Port Sonochan Hotel, and was probably broken up in around 1895. *Countess of Breadalbane* is visible in the distance.

Countess of Breadalbane was built in 1882 by Hannah & Donald of Paisley for Duncan Fraser, who was the proprietor of the Lochawe Hotel. She also ran from Lochawe pier to Ford. She was re-engined twice, in 1884 and 1898. Both sets of machinery, a compound and a triple expansion respectively, came from Hawthorn & Co. of Leith.

Countess of Breadalbane was laid up in 1914 and was taken over by the Caledonian Steam Packet Co. Ltd in 1922. She is seen here at Ford pier in a unique photograph, in the 'tartan lum' colour scheme, the yellow, red and black funnel colours of 1923-24.

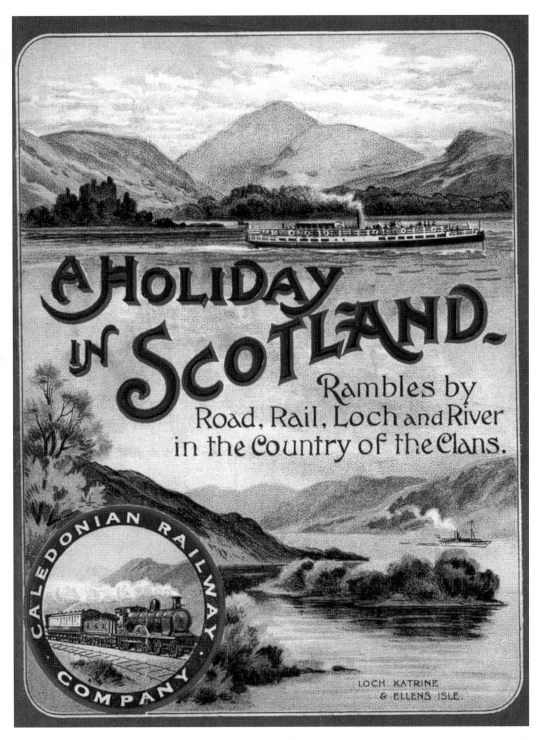

A HOLIDAY IN SCOTLAND.

Rambles by
Road, Rail, Loch and River
in the Country of the Clans.

CALEDONIAN RAILWAY COMPANY

LOCH KATRINE
& ELLENS ISLE.

The cover of a Caledonian Railway booklet featuring day tours from Glasgow depicts *Countess of Breadalbane* at the top, with a poor representation of *Sir Walter Scott* at the bottom.

Countess of Breadalbane, seen here leaving Port Sonachan, continued on the loch until she was broken up in 1936 and replaced by her successor of the same name. Her deckhouse survives as a garden shed at Connel. (CRSC)

Caledonia was built in 1895 for the Port Sonachan Hotel. She was constructed by Bow McLachlan of Paisley in sections, and was erected on the shores of the loch. She was a twin-screw steamer with two sets of compound engines. In 1918 she was sold for service in Belgium. She was dismantled at Port Sonachan and taken to Lochawe pier on a barge, with the boiler towed behind the barge. It was intended that she be lengthened, but no work was done, and she was broken up where she lay.

CAMERON'S
GLEN NANT
AND THE
FALLS OF BLAIRGOUR
CIRCULAR TOUR
By Caledonian Railway,
FOUR-IN-HAND COACHES,
AND THE
S.S. "CALEDONIA,"

Via Taynuilt, Glen Nant, Portsonachan, Falls of Blairgour, Loch Awe,
Kilchurn Castle and the Pass of Brander,

Daily from Oban at 9.40 a.m, and 12.35 p.m.

	1st Class and Cabin,	3rd Class and Cabin,
Fares for the Round, ...	11s. 9d.	10s. 3d.
Fares not including the Falls, ...	9s. 0d.	7s. 6d.

Tickets issued and all information given at CAMERON'S Glen Nant Booking Office, Esplanade, Oban ; or at the Railway Stations.

An undated advertisement from a guidebook for a circular tour from Oban. It involved a sail on *Caledonia*, from Taychreggan to Lochawe pier.

Growley was a steam launch used for short trips from Lochawe pier. She had been built by Scott's Shipbuilding and Engineering of Greenock. She had been originally used by Mr Scott as a yacht from his house at Eredine, near the south end of Loch Awe. In 1900 she was purchased by Duncan Fraser of the Lochawe Hotel, and remained in service until 1936. She is seen here in a 1935 photograph at Loch Awe pier with Kilchurn Castle in the background.

CIRCULAR TOUR
LOCH AWE
AND
PASS OF MELFORT

'DAILY (except Sundays)

Ceases after 18th SEPTEMBER, 1948

Going by Train via Pass of Brander to Loch Awe; Motor Vessel " Countess of Breadalbane " on Loch Awe to Ford, thence Messrs. Alexander's Motor to Oban, via Pass of Melfort.

or the route may be reversed

GOING VIA PASS OF BRANDER			GOING VIA PASS OF MELFORT		
		a.m.			a.m.
OBAN............Train	leave	9 12	OBAN...............Motor	leave	11 0
CONNEL FERRY ... „	„	9 30	FORD .... „	arrive	12 45p
TAYNUILT .... „	„	9 43	FORD ....Motor Vessel	leave	1 0
LOCH AWE .... „	arrive	10 1	LOCH AWE ...... „	arrive	3 20
LOCH AWE ....Motor Vessel	leave 10 10		LOCH AWE ......Train	leave	3 42
FORD .... „	arrive	12 30p	TAYNUILT .... „	arrive	4 0
FORD ....Motor	leave	1 0	CONNEL FERRY „	„	4 20
OBAN............. „	arrive	2 45	OBAN............... „	„	4 37

FARES FOR THE ROUND

FIRST CLASS	From	THIRD CLASS
s. d.	OBAN	s. d.
20 3	CONNEL FERRY TAYNUILT LOCH AWE	**18 5**

The Tickets are valid for three calendar months from Date of Issue and for break of journey at any point en route.

LUNCHEON AND TEAS CAN BE OBTAINED ON BOARD THE MOTOR VESSEL, WHICH IS FULLY LICENSED.

Above: In 1936, the LMSR introduced a new motor vessel to Loch Awe. The second *Countess of Breadalbane* was built by Denny of Dumbarton and was erected on the slipway which was half a mile from Lochawe Station. She was launched on 7 May 1936 and entered service on 1 June. She made a daily sailing from Loch Awe pier to Ford with calls, in her first season at least, at Taychreggan and Portsonochan. (CRSC)

Left: Countess of Breadalbane was laid up on the slipway from the outbreak of war in 1939, until June 1948. This handbill from the latter season shows the Loch Awe and Pass of Melfort circular tour, which was operated from Oban by train to Loch Awe, steamer to Ford, and bus back to Oban. (G.E. Langmuir Collection, Mitchell Library, Glasgow)

Right: In the post-war years, *Countess of Breadalbane* offered a non-landing afternoon cruise from Loch Awe pier, which is shown in this 1949 handbill. The outward rail connection from Glasgow was by the short-lived service from Glasgow (Queen Street) via the West Highland line to Crianlarich, and thence to Oban by the Callander and Oban Line. (G.E. Langmuir Collection, Mitchell Library, Glasgow)

Below: On 20 April 1952, *Countess of Breadalbane* was moved by road to Loch Fyne, for her new career on the Clyde. She is seen here being taken over the Callander and Oban Railway near Loch Awe pier. Her subsequent career on the Clyde is covered in *Caledonia Steam Packet Company Ltd.* By 1981 she was named *Countess of Kempock*, and started a new career on Loch Lomond as *Countess Fiona* (see pp. 63–68). (CRSC)

BRITISH RAILWAYS

B. 1438.

CHEAP DAY EXCURSION
TO
LOCH AWE

WITH TWO HOURS CRUISE ON LOCH

By Motor Vessel "COUNTESS OF BREADALBANE"

On TUESDAYS, WEDNESDAYS and THURSDAYS

5th JULY until 8th SEPTEMBER, 1949

TRAIN

	B a.m.
GLASGOW (Queen Street) ....leave	9.31
HELENSBURGH (Upper) .... „	10.15
LOCH AWE STATION ....arrive	12.12p

MOTOR VESSEL

LOCH AWE PIER ....leave	3.40
LOCH AWE PIER ....arrive	5.40

TRAIN

	R	B
LOCH AWE STATION ....leave	6.8	7.15
HELENSBURGH (Upper) .... „	—	9.15
GLASGOW (Buchanan Street) ....arrive	9.31	—
GLASGOW (Queen Street) .... „	—	9.56

B Conveys Buffet Car.   R Conveys Restaurant Car.

From GLASGOW		DAY RETURN FARES	From HELENSBURGH	
1st Class	3rd Class		1st Class	3rd Class
30/-	20/-		23/9d	16/3d

THE TICKETS ARE VALID ONLY ON DAY OF ISSUE BY THE SERVICES SPECIFIED AND CAN BE OBTAINED IN ADVANCE AT STATIONS.

NOTE.—Teas can be obtained on board the Motor Vessel, which is fully licensed.

Children under three years of age, free; three years and under fourteen, half fare.
CONDITIONS OF ISSUE.—The Tickets are issued subject to the conditions applicable to Tickets of this description as shown in the Notices issued by the Railway Executive.
All information regarding Excursions and Cheap Fares will be supplied on application at Stations or to Mr H. R. STATHAM, District Commercial Superintendent, 50 George Square, Glasgow. Telephone No. Douglas 7080.
July, 1949.
E.R.O. 53302.   (SS 9559 M IS M)

20M—30/6/49—No. 1.   Herald Press, Arbroath

Steam returned to Loch Awe in 1986 in the form of the launch *Lady Rowena*. She had been built with a diesel engine in 1927, and was named *Water Lily* for service on Lake Windermere. She had had a varied career until Harry Watson purchased her in 1984. A replica Sisson compound steam engine was fitted, with a boiler powered by wood or peat, thus making her the only peat-powered steam vessel in the world.

Lady Rowena was advertised by a large cut-out picture of her on the roadside. She entered service on the loch in 1986 for the Dalriada Steam Packet Co. Ltd. She ran from Loch Awe pier on a variety of trips, with some of them going down the loch to Dalavich, Portsonachan, Taychreggan and Ardanaiseag Hotel. In 1988 a railway carriage was purchased and was used at Loch Awe pier as a tea room and waiting room.

Right: The steam engine of *Lady Rowena.* Sadly, Harry Watson died in 1992, but the operation of the steamer was continued by his widow, Averil. From 1996 onwards, calls were made at Kilchurn Castle, and the service became mainly a ferry from Loch Awe pier to there.

Below: The foredeck of *Lady Rowena.* In 1999 she was sold to the Ardanaiseag Hotel and the Loch Awe Steam Packet Company was formed to operate her and *Flower of Scotland.* In around 2000 or 2001, *Lady Rowena* sank at her moorings, but returned to service in September 2003.

In 1991, the waterbus-type vessel, *Flower of Scotland*, entered service on the loch. She had been built in 1978 for service at Tenby as *Pili Pala*, and had later operated at Runnymede on the Thames as *The New Princess of Wales*. She now maintains the ferry service to Kilchurn Castle.

A board gives details of the ferry service to Kilchurn Castle offered by *Flower of Scotland*.

four
Loch Etive

Steamer and Coach at Pier, Loch Etive.

In being a sea loch, Loch Etive is unlike the other lochs featured in this book. Access to the sea is by the narrows at Connel which, at certain states of the tide, become rapids known as the Falls of Lora. Because of this, the passenger services on the loch have generally been self-contained. *Ossian*, which is shown here at Lochtivehead, was the third steamer to run on Loch Etive. The first was *Ben Starav*, which ran from 1877 to 1879 and was a former yacht. The second was *Glenetive*, which ran from 1880 until the arrival of *Ossian* in 1886.

Ossian ran from Achnacloich pier, which is seen here. It was adjacent to a station on the Callander & Oban Railway, and had an intermediate call at Taynuilt to Lochetivehead and a connecting horse coach to Ballachulish. She was built by T.B. Seath of Rutherglen, who also supplied her compound engines.

Above: Ossian at Lochetivehead, with the connecting coach for Ballachulish station. She was withdrawn in 1913 and sold to Turkish owners. She was apparently used as a baggage boat on the Bosphorus, and was taken over by the Turkish Navy as a tender in the First World War. *Below left:* An undated advertisement from a contemporary guidebook for the Loch Etive circular tour, which features *Ossian. Below right:* Loch Etive sailings were resumed in 1922 with the motor launch *Jano*, and from 1923 to 1941 by another motor launch named *Lochetive Queen*. By this time the coach connection to Ballachulish was by motor charabanc. Other boats used in the inter-war years were named *Rena* and *Euglena*.

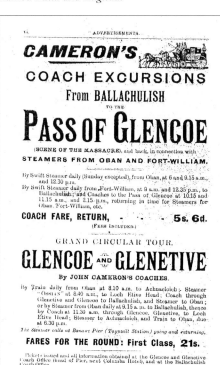

1946

The Far-Famed Pass of Glencoe,
Glen Etive, and Loch Etive
CIRCULAR TOUR

Passing through the Scene of the Massacre

THE PREMIER TOUR OF THE HIGHLANDS
UNRIVALLED FOR GRANDEUR OF SCENERY

By Train, Motor Coach, and Luxurious Passenger Yacht
DARTHULA II, viewing the Wildest and Grandest
Mountain and Loch Scenery in the Highlands, and is the
only means of doing Glencoe, Glen Etive and Loch Etive
FROM 1st JUNE UNTIL 28th SEPTEMBER

Views of Special and Historical Interest described during the Journey

GOING via BALLACHULISH			GOING via ACHNACLOICH		
and Returning via Achnacloich			and Returning via Ballachulish		
Passengers join Motor Coaches at Ballachulish Glencoe (terminus) Station			OBAN	train leaves	9.50 a.m.
OBAN	train leaves	9.50 a.m.	ACHNACLOICH	,, arrives	10.17 a.m.
BALLACHULISH	,, arrives	11.13 a.m.	do.	yacht leaves	10.30 a.m.
do.	motor leaves	11.30 a.m.	LOCHETIVEHEAD	,, arrives	12.30 p.m.
LOCHETIVEHEAD	,, arrives	1.20 p.m.	do.	motor leaves	1.30 p.m.
do.	boat leaves	2. 0 p.m.	BALLACHULISH	,, arrives	3.55 p.m.
OBAN	train arrives	4.38 p.m.	OBAN	train arrives	5.36 p.m.

Lunch and Teas on board Boat at Moderate Charges (Fully Licensed). Motor Coach calls at New Hotel, Glencoe, in each direction, allowing time for Light Refreshments only.

INCLUSIVE FARES FOR TOUR

	FIRST CLASS	THIRD CLASS		FIRST CLASS	THIRD CLASS
Appin	17 0	13 8	Creagan	16 10	13 8
Ballachulish (Glencoe) ...	16 9	13 6	Dalmally	24 9	18 4
Ballachulish (Ferry)	16 10	13 8	Loch Awe ... ... '... ...	23 3	17 7
Benderloch	16 11	13 9	Oban	19 10	15 7
Connel Ferry	16 10	13 8	Taynuilt	18 6	14 8

" OBAN TIMES " LTD.

Left: Darthula II was built in 1939 for the circular tour advertised in this handbill, and resumed service after the war in 1946, continuing until 1963.

Below: Darthula II features in this postcard view. She was sold in 1964 for service on the Thames. She was later at Portsmouth and may still be in existence there, although in very poor condition.

Darthula II was replaced in 1964 by *Shearwater*, which was a wartime-built Fairmile launch. She was quickly renamed *Etive Shearwater*, and initially offered non-landing cruises. However, she made calls at Lochetivehead in the 1966 season, although the connecting buses which had ceased after the withdrawal of *Darthula II* in 1963 did not resume. In 1967 she was sold for use at Ullapool and later moved to Arisaig, where she operated for many years to the Small Isles, until she was withdrawn after the summer of 2002. She is seen here at Achnacloich in 1965, with the motor yacht *Caterina* inboard of her. *Caterina* was used as a restaurant on the pier in the early part of the 1965 season, and later in the year did offer some cruises. She had been built in 1924 by George Brown & Co. of Greenock.

After a break of two years without sailings, *Jessie Ellen* was introduced to the loch in 1970. She ran from Taynuilt, as Achnacloich pier and the adjacent station were now closed and offered non-landing cruises. She had formerly sailed on Loch Ness (see page 127) and later moved to Orkney. (CRSC)

Anne of Etive arriving at Taynuilt. She was built in 1975 for the cruises on Loch Etive, and is currently in service. She offers three cruises daily in the summer. There are two ninety-minute cruises in the morning which take passengers to see the seals on the islets off Inverlever, and also a three-hour afternoon non-landing cruise to the head of the loch.

Anne of Etive at Taynuilt. Her sailings are well patronised, and give passengers a chance to see the otherwise inaccessible scenery, and sometimes glimpses of golden eagles as well as seals.

Anne of Etive still functions as a supply boat, and serves remote settlements on the loch shore. Here a crew member is rowing ashore on an inflatable boat. He has three boxes of groceries at his feet, and some mail for an isolated house on the loch's edge.

five

Loch Katrine

Tourists have come to Loch Katrine since the early part of the nineteenth century, following the publication of Sir Walter Scott's *The Lady of the Lake* in 1810. Transport on the loch was initially by a large rowing boat named *Waterwitch*. In 1843 the small paddle steamer *Gipsy* was purchased for service on the loch. She had initially run as an experimental craft on the Forth and Clyde Canal, and was conveyed from Stirling to Loch Katrine on a horse-drawn wagon. It took more than ten days to drag her from Callander, with various long stops of a day or more due to the wagon wheels sinking into the muddy road. The horses bolted in the final mile or two before the loch, and it took several days to catch them. She only operated for a week or so, then disappeared one night from her moorings, at what is now Trossachs pier. It was assumed that the boatmen from the rowing boat had untied her, taken her to the deepest part of the loch below Ben Venue, and had then sunk her. Several of the boatmen were taken to court, but they all professed to speak only in Gaelic and the case was found 'not proven'. However, they could converse perfectly well in English with their passengers.

In 1845, the paddle steamer *Rob Roy* was built by William Denny for the New Lochlomond Steamboat Company, for service on Loch Katrine. She was steamed up to Inversnaid. It was intended that she would be dragged across to Loch Katrine on a cradle wagon, but that proved impossible, and she was cut into eight sections and taken across. She was then re-assembled at Coalbarns, which is now Stronachlachar. She entered service in 1846, by which time she was owned by a new company. Half of the shares were owned by the Lochlomond Steamboat Company, and half by the tenants of the Trossachs Inn. She lasted in service until 1854. An 1856 plan to convert her to a screw steamer and take her to Loch Tay was abandoned, and she was sold in 1859 for use as a workboat for the contractors working on the new waterworks scheme. She was later sunk in the loch.

In 1855, a second *Rob Roy*, which was this time a screw steamer, was built. The above advertisement was for her first season, sailing from the Trossachs, or Stirling End to Coalbarns, or Loch Lomond End.

Above: This is the second *Rob Roy* in her early condition with two masts, at Trossachs pier.

Below: Rob Roy at Coalbarns, which is the first pier at Stronachlachar. The photograph is from a G. Washington Wilson album with an owner's inscription dated 1871. This pier and the adjacent hotel were abandoned after the raising of the water level in 1895.

Rob Roy at Trossachs pier.

P. S. "Rob Roy", Loch Katrine.

With love from Marie.

In later years, *Rob Roy* had her deckhouses, boiler casing and saloon companionway painted white.

Rob Roy, again at Trossachs pier. The thatched shelter was there before the present shelter. Later her funnel was painted yellow with a black top, which is seen in this 'moonlit' view.

In her final years, *Rob Roy* had her funnel painted yellow to match *Sir Walter Scott*. She is seen here at the lay by the mooring where she spent much of her time from 1900, when *Sir Walter Scott* was introduced, until her scuttling around 1911.

A full *Rob Roy* off Ellen's Isle.

A postcard view shows the old pier at Trossachs. The small steam launch *MacGregor*, which served the large houses on the loch shore, is on the right.

In 1899, a new steamer, *Sir Walter Scott*, was built for Loch Katrine. She was ordered from Mathew Paul of Dumbarton, who sub-contracted the hull to William Denny & Bros, and was fitted with a triple expansion engine. She is seen here in her original condition, with no wheelhouse. The wheel on the deck is forward of the funnel.

Sir Walter Scott in her original condition at the second pier at Stronachlachar, in front of the hotel. She was initially difficult to steer because her steersman could not see ahead when she was full of passengers. In 1902 her wheel was raised to give him a better view.

Sir Walter Scott at Trossachs pier, prior to the scuttling of *Rob Roy* in 1911.

In 1909, the golden jubilee of the Loch Katrine Water Scheme was celebrated by an illuminated Glasgow Corporation tram.

Sir Walter Scott, after the fitting of a bridge. She is with *MacGregor* at Trossachs pier.

This is Trossachs pier *c.* 1925. The picture shows *Sir Walter Scott*, charabancs in the car park, and a horse bus about to depart for Callander or Aberfoyle.

Sir Walter Scott in a 1930s view, just after leaving Trossachs pier, with a large collection of parked cars and buses. She was laid up during the war years, and was in very poor condition at the end of it, but fortunately was returned to service. This area now has a souvenir shop in the building behind the buses, and the 'Captain's Rest' café to the right.

Sir Walter Scott at the present pier at Stronachlachar, prior to her wheelhouse being fitted.

STEAMER AT LOCH KATRINE PIER, TROSSACHS.

B.6566

A full *Sir Walter Scott* about to depart from Trossachs pier, after her wheelhouse was fitted in the late 1940s, but prior to 1956 when her saloon windows were replaced by portholes. The pier to the right was used to re-boiler the steamer in 1956.

Sir Walter Scott on the loch after 1956. In 1956 she was re-boilered and portholes replaced her saloon windows. Eglinton Hotels Ltd owned the Loch Katrine Steamboat Co. and also had hotels at Inversnaid, Stronachlachar and Callander. They owned *Sir Walter Scott* until she was taken over by the Glasgow Corporation Water Department in 1953.

Sir Walter Scott approaching Trossachs pier in August 1966.

In 1969, the Glasgow Corporation Water Department, including the Loch Katrine steamer and tea room, became part of the Lower Clyde water board. At this time *Sir Walter Scott*'s funnel was painted white. She is seen here, unusually bow in, at Trossachs pier in 1981. The ownership passed to Strathclyde Regional Council in 1975, to West of Scotland Water in 1997, and to Scottish Water in 2002, due to various reorganisations of local government and water authorities.

Sir Walter Scott with all flags flying at Trossachs pier in 1990, on the occasion of a ninetieth birthday charter for the Clyde River Steamer Club.

Sir Walter Scott arriving at Trossachs pier in her centenary year, 2000.

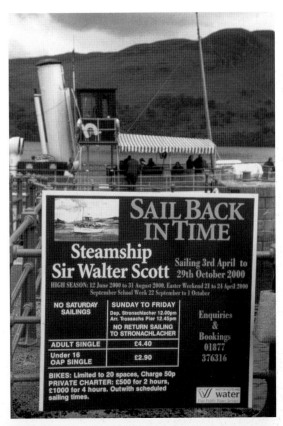

Right: Sir Walter Scott was promoted in 2000 under the slogan, 'Sail back in time'. At the time of the withdrawal of *Maid of the Loch* in 1981, her afternoon cruise to Stronachlachar had been replaced by two shorter non-landing cruises, which were mainly aimed at the coach tour trade.

Below: The triple expansion machinery of *Sir Walter Scott*. She continues to steam on Loch Katrine after 103 years. Her season has been lengthened in recent years and she now sails from Easter to the end of October.

Sir Walter Scott arriving at Stronachlachar on the occasion of her centenary cruise, which was organised by the Clyde River Steamer Club in June 2000.

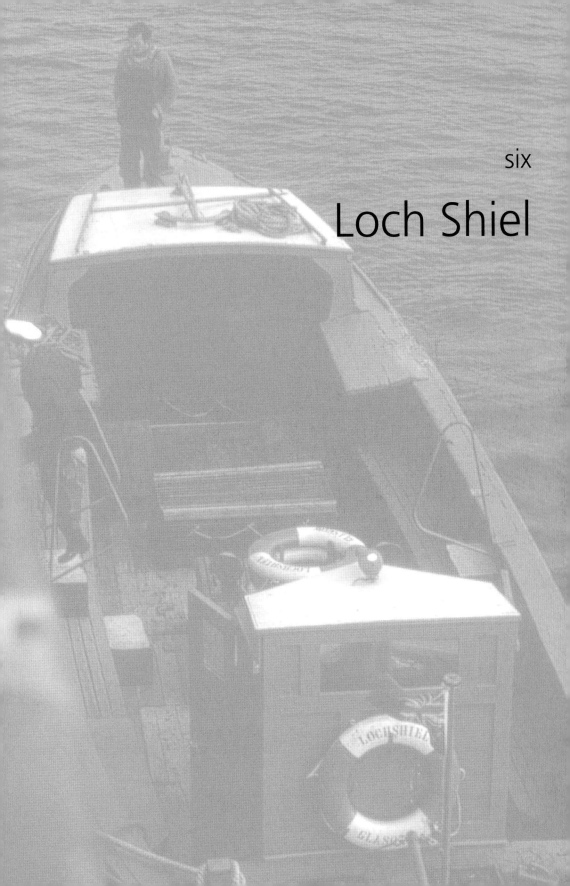

six

Loch Shiel

In 1893 the first steamer appeared on Loch Shiel. This was the small steam launch *Maud*, which was owned by David MacBrayne. She had been built as a steam yacht by T.B. Seath & Co. at Rutherglen and purchased by MacBrayne in 1889. She ran on the loch until 1897, making a weekly trip from Shiel Bridge, where MacBrayne owned a hotel, to Glenfinnan. She was otherwise used for towing boats of fishermen around the loch.

Lady of the Lake had been the yacht of Lord Howard of Glossop, who was one of the local landowners, and she commenced a service in 1898. She had been built at Dartmouth in 1894 and ran from Moss pier at Shiel Bridge to Glenfinnan. She was used as a relief to *Clanranald II* in later years, then was dieselised in 1936, and finally sank at her moorings in the winter of 1951-52.

In September 1898, a new twin screw steamer was ordered from T.B. Seath & Co. for the loch. *Clanranald* was delivered in April 1899 but her draught was too deep for the trip up the river Callop to Glenfinnan pier. In 1902 she was sold for use as a yacht, and renamed *Madge*. She then became *Hinba* in 1922. She was lost off the coastline of the Gold Coast, which is now Ghana, on 26 November 1924. In 1900 *Clanranald II* arrived on the loch. Seath built her, with machinery by J. Fisher & Co. She was a foot beamier than her predecessor and drew five inches less water. (From *Clyde Steamers* magazine)

Here *Clanranald II* is off Glenfinnan in a postcard view, which shows the monument to Bonnie Prince Charlie. The opening of the West Highland Extension Railway from Fort William to Mallaig in 1901 brought much more business to the loch. The pier at the south end was changed from Shiel Bridge to Acharacle, on the other side of the loch, in 1901, at which time a pier opened at Dalilea. Other piers were later built at Glenaladale, Polloch, and Achanellan. In 1909 *Clanranald II* was awarded a Royal Mail contract for the service.

In November 1921 the Loch Shiel Steamboat Company took over the service on the loch, which had previously been operated by Lord Howard of Glossop as a private venture. In 1925 *Clanranald II* was steamed to Oban and converted to a motor ship. She is seen here at her berth in the River Callop after being converted. She was withdrawn in October 1953, and was broken up at Acharacle in the following year. (From *Clyde Steamers* magazine)

In 1951, the loch service and mail contract was taken over by David MacBrayne Ltd. They built two launches for the loch service, to be named *Rosalind* and *Celia*. At the same time, a new pier was built at Glenfinnan, near Glenfinnan House Hotel. In view of objections to the proposed names, it was decided instead to call them *Lochshiel* and *Lochailort* respectively. *Lochailort* is seen here off Acharacle in September 1954. (From *Clyde Steamers* magazine)

Clockwise from top left:

In 1962, *Lochshiel* was transferred to the Fionnphort to Iona service and is seen here in 1969 tendering to *King George V.* On 28 April 1970, while on her way back to the Clyde for overhaul, she was struck by an unidentified ship off Holy Isle, and was sunk.

   Lochailort was withdrawn after the 1967 season. She was transferred to Kyle of Lochalsh in June 1968 for the Kyle to Toscaig service, but her hull was condemned the following year and she was burnt on the shore at Kyle.

From 1968 to the 1980s the open motor launch *Rose Isle* offered cruises on the loch.

In April 1998, the launch *Sileas*, which was built in 1940 as an admiralty harbour launch, entered service on the loch. She is moored off the Glenfinnan Hotel in this picture. She makes a weekly trip right down the loch to Acharacle, and shorter trips on the remaining days of the week. She came into civilian ownership in the mid-1960s at Invergordon. Later she was given the name *Vital Spark*, and operated from Kyle of Lochalsh to Toscaig, under contract to David MacBrayne Ltd. In 1987 she was sold for use out of Ullapool, and from 1990 to 1994 ran from Ulva Ferry on Mull to Iona, Staffa and the Treshnish Isles. In 1996 she was purchased by her present owner, who spent almost all of 1997 restoring her.

seven

Loch Tay

From top:

In 1882, the Loch Tay Steamboat Company was formed by the Earl of Breadalbane. One passenger steamer and one cargo steamer were built in that year for the service from Kenmore to Killin. The passenger steamer was named *Lady of the Lake*, and is shown on this postcard. She was built at Kenmore by Anderson and Lyall of Govan, with compound machinery by D. Rowan and Sons. She served on the loch until 1928, when she was broken up at Kenmore.

The cargo steamer was named *Sybilla*. She is shown here at Kenmore pier with *Lady of the Lake* across the end of the pier. The aft cabin was a later addition and she was not originally built with this. She was wooden-hulled and was built at Kenmore by D. Fenton of Perth, also with machinery by Rowan. In 1884 a new compound engine replaced her original simple expansion one. She was broken up at Kenmore in 1929. Two additional cargo steamers, *Magpie* and *Carlotta*, also served on the loch. *Magpie* served from 1882, until she sunk in a storm in 1907, and *Carlotta* served from 1883 to 1923.

In 1907 the twin-screw steamer *Queen of the Lake* entered service. She was built by Ailsa Shipbuilding of Troon and taken in sections by rail to Killin. There, she was loaded onto a barge and towed by *Sybilla* to Dalerb near Kenmore, where she was erected.

120

178 *Steamers and Railways.*

LOCH TAY STEAMERS.

Sailings for July, August, and September of Royal Mail Steamers, showing Railway and Coach Connections.

STATIONS.		p.m.		p.m.
London, Euston, leaves		8 50		10 0
Do. St Pancras „		8 25		9 15
Do. King's Cross „		8 40		8 40
		a.m.		a.m.
Carlisle, N.B. . „				4 52
Do. Cal. . „		4 32		6 10
Edin., *via* Stirling „		6 48		8 30
Do. *via* Fife . „		6 35		
Glasgow, Buch. St. „		7 10		9 0
Stirling . . „		8 9		10 2
Oban . . . „		..		5 25
Callander . . „		7 50		8 30
Dundee, West . „		7 40		11 5
Perth, Highland . „		9 30		11 50
Aberdeen . . „				8 55
Inverness . . „		6 0		10 10
Aberfeldy . . arrives		10 55		3 5
		a.m.		p.m.
Coach leaves Aberfeldy		11 0		3 15
STEAMER.	Pas. a.m.	Pas. Exp. p.m.	Pas. and Mail p.m.	Pas. p.m.
Kenmore Pier leave	7 40	12 15	1 30	4 30
Fernan . . „	7 55	..	1 45	4 45
Ardtalnaig . „	8 15	..	2 5	5 5
Lawers . . „	8 20	..	2 10	5 10
Ardeonaig . „	8 35	..	2 25	5 25
Killin Pier arrive	9 40	1 55	3 30	6 30
STATIONS.	a.m.	p.m.	p.m.	p.m.
Loch Tay (Killin Pier) l'ves	9 46	2 5	3 36	6 52
Killin . . . {arr.	..	2 9	..	6 56
{l'vs.	9 50	2 26	3 40	7 12
Killin Junction, arrives	10 4	2 40	3 54	7 25
Oban . Train arrives	12 20	6 17	6 17	9 43
Callander „	11 4	3 45	7 20	9 30
Perth . „	3 20	6 40	9 20	11 30
Dundee, West „	4 45	7 30	10 30	12 40
Aberdeen „	8 30	10 0	3 20	3 20
Stirling . „	11 54	4 37	8 12	10 28
Edin., Wav. „	1 50	6 30	9 55	..
Glas., Buch. St. „	1 25	5 43	9 15	11 30
Carlisle, Cal. „	5 17	8 35	11 57	..
Do. N.B. „	5 20	11 54	..	..
	a.m.	a.m.	a.m.	
L don, King's Cross „	2 15	5 45	8 15	..
Do. St. Pancras „	4 15	7 10	8 25	..
Do. Euston „	3 50	3 50	7 45	..

STATIONS.	a.m.	p.m.	p.m.	n't
London, Euston leaves		8 50	10 0	12 0
Do. St Pancras „		8 25	9 15	..
Do. King's Cross „		8 40	8 40	..
		a.m.	a m.	a.m.
Carlisle, N.B. . „		..	4 52	8 15
Do. Cal. . „		4 32	6 10	9 25
				p.m.
Glasgow, Buch. Street „		7 10	9 20	1 15
Edinburgh, Wav'ley „		6 43	8 30	12 25
Stirling . . „		8 15	10 20	2 14
Aberdeen . . „		..	..	8 55
Dundee, West . „		6 20	7 40	11 5
Perth . . „		7 30	8 30	12 0
Callander . . „		9 17	11 20	3 10
Oban . . . „	5 25	8 5	p.m.	12 40
Killin Junction . „	7 40	10 20	12 23	4 12
Killin . . . {arr.	7 54		12 37	
{l'vs.	9 0	10 34	1 50	4 26
Loch Tay (Killin Pier) arr.	9 5	10 38	1 55	4 30
STEAMER.	Pas. a.m.	Pas. and Mail. a.m.	Pas. Exp. p.m.	Pas. p.m.
Killin Pier leave	9 10	10 45	2 10	4 35
Ardeonaig „	9 35	11 10	..	5 0
Lawers „	9 50	11 25	..	5 15
Ardtalnaig „	10 0	11 30	..	5 20
Fernan „	10 20	11 50	..	5 40
		p.m.		
Kenmore arrive	11 10	12 45	3 50	6 35
STATIONS.	a.m.	p.m.		p.m.
Kenmore, Coach leaves	11 15	3 50		6 40
	p.m.			7 40
Aberfeldy, „ arrives	12 15	4 50		A Train leaves Aberfeldy on Fridays at 8 p.m. for Pitlochry and Blair-Athole.
Aberfeldy, N., Train leaves	12 20	4 55		
Inverness, „ „ arrives	6 5	10 5		
Aberfeldy, S., „ leaves	1 55	4 55		
Perth . . . arrive	3 33	6 45		
Dundee . . . „	4 45	7 30		
Aberdeen . . „	8 30	10 0		
Callander . . „	5 35	11 45		
		a.m.		
Oban . . . „	9 43	4 15		
		p.m.		
Stirling . . . „	4 57	8 21		
Glas., Buch. St. . „	6 0	9 25		
Edin. *via* Stirling . „	6 30	9 55		
Do. *via* Fife . „	7 20	10 0		
Carlisle, N.B. . „	11 54	..		
Do. Cal. . . „	8 35	11 57		
	a.m.	a.m		
London, King's Cross „	5 45	8 15		
Do. St Pancras „	7 10	8 25		
Do. Euston „	3 50	7 45		

In addition to above, a Coach will leave Kenmore daily at 8.30 a.m.; returning from Aberfeldy at 1.40 p.m., and 6.15 p.m. The Steamers are intended to sail as above, weather and other circumstances permitting. The Proprietor does not guarantee the Railway and Coach runnings shown on this page, as he has no control over them. Passengers, Live Stock, and Goods by the Loch Tay Steamers are carried solely at Owner's risk.

*** For particulars of train alterations during the season, see Time Tables issued by the different Companies.

Passengers are requested to look after their own LUGGAGE, as the Steamer will not be responsible.

WM. J. FRASER, Manager.

. . LOCH TAY STEAMERS . .

Popular Excursion to KILLIN PIER and BACK

IN ONE DAY From Stations on the Highland Railway, affording a : : Pleasure Sail : : on LOCH - TAY, the most famous and lovely : : Loch in Scotland. : :

The MOST DIRECT ROUTE to OBAN and FORT-WILLIAM

VIA ABERFELDY AND LOCH-TAY

Tourists by this New and Beautiful Route have opportunities daily for travelling to and from OBAN and FORT-WILLIAM

CHEAP EXCURSION FARES

Tourists Tickets issued daily by Morning Trains from Highland Stations to Killin Pier and Back via Aberfeldy.

For full particulars as to Trains, Motors, and Steamer Sailings, see Time-Tables and Monthly Steamboat Sailing Bills, etc., to apply to THE MANAGER,

LOCH TAY STEAMBOAT Co., Ltd.,
KENMORE.

Clockwise from top left:

An undated pre-1923 Loch Tay timetable shows connections from many towns and cities, and four daily sailings in each direction on the loch. A coach connection from Aberfeldy to Kenmore brought passengers at the eastern end, whilst the Killin branch line extended to Loch Tay pier.

An advertisement for the Loch Tay Steamboat Company for excursions from Kenmore. The steamers did not operate in the 1921 summer, and in 1922 the company was taken over by the Caledonian Railway.

Queen of the Lake at Kenmore. She was laid up on the slipway at Kenmore at the start of the Second World War in 1939 and never sailed again, as she was sold for scrapping where she lay in 1950.

Passenger train services were cut back from Loch Tay pier to Killin in 1939 when the steamer service ceased, although the line remained in operation as the engine shed was at Loch Tay pier. Caledonian Railway 0-4-4 tanks continued to be in use until the early 1960s, as in this view of Killin station. (David Deayton)

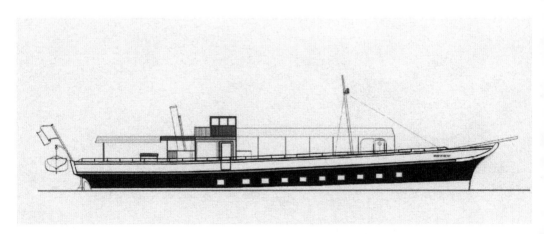

In 2003 plans were announced for a new steamer, *Spirit of the Tay*, to be built for excursions on Loch Tay from Kenmore. She was built in sections at Ferguson's yard at Port Glasgow and was fitted with a Crabtree engine. Her profile is similar to the Loch Katrine steamer, *Rob Roy,* of 1855. The sections were taken by road from Port Glasgow to Dalferb for re-erection in November 2003. It is expected she will enter service in summer 2004.

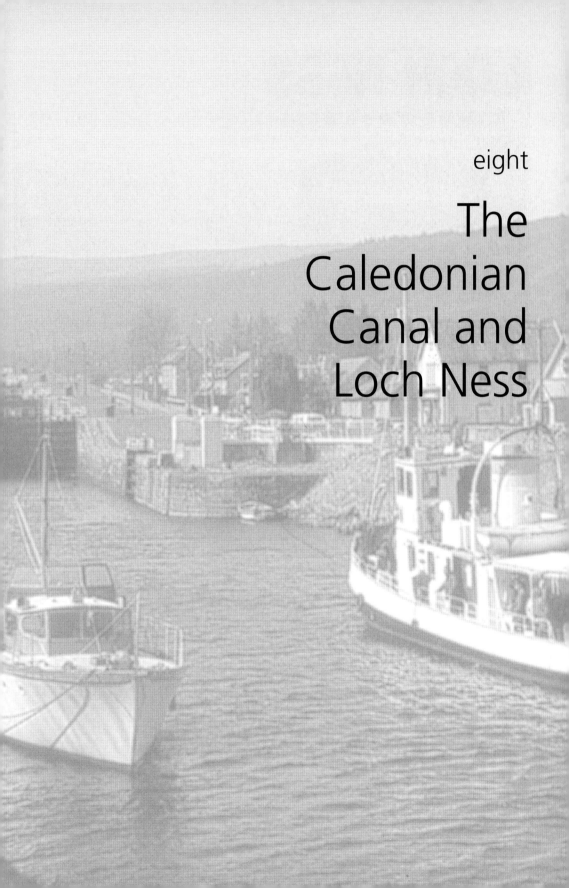

eight

The Caledonian Canal and Loch Ness

The services on Loch Ness and the Caledonian Canal operated by MacBrayne prior to the Second World War are dealt with in *MacBrayne Steamers*. A variety of post-war operators are dealt with here.

Above left: In 1948 and 1949, Lochness Cruises Ltd operated the Fairmile launch *Lenrodian* on cruises out of Muirtown Lock, Inverness. She had been built in 1942 by a firm named Curtis and her name represented the three shareholders of the company: Len Wilkinson, Rod Smart and Ian MacDonald.

Above right: In 1958, the motor launch *Cramond Brig* operated cruises from Muirtown Lock. She had been built at Sandhaven in 1921, and had originally operated for SMT out of South Queensferry, and from 1934 under charter between Largs and Millport. After leaving Loch Ness she passed to owners at Leith and later at Campbeltown. She was wrecked on 21 January 1966.

Cruises on the
CALEDONIAN CANAL
and LOCH NESS

Home of the famous "monster"

M.V. SCOT II
'Round Trip' Cruises from Inverness
DAILY (exc. Sundays) THROUGH THE SEASON

From INVERNESS, Top of Muirtown Locks

By Car—Take A.9 Dingwall Road to Canal Swing Bridge, one-and-a-quarter miles from town centre and turn sharp left over bridge. Car Park at Departure Quay.

By Bus—Dalneigh bus from Academy Street (near Railway Station). Cross over Canal by lock gates.

CALEDONIAN CANAL — BRITISH WATERWAYS BOARD
1971

[p.t.o]

Right: In late 1960, British Waterways converted their steam icebreaking tug, *Scot II*, which had been built at Leith in 1931, to a motor passenger vessel. She commenced thrice daily cruises from Inverness the following summer. These continued until 1991.

Below: Scot II approaching Fort Augustus Locks in a postcard view. It was taken on the occasion of a Coastal Cruising Association charter along the length of the Caledonian Canal from Inverness to Banavie, on 2 September 1972.

Scot II at her berth in Inverness. After her withdrawal she was in use as a floating pub near Laggan Locks for a time.

More recently, *Scot II* has been returned to Inverness for refurbishment and a planned return to cruising. In early 2003 her existing superstructure was replaced, and the modified vessel is shown in this photograph taken at Muirtown basin in June 2003. (Steven)

Right: From 1961 to 1966, the wooden launch *Jessie Ellen* offered competition to *Scot II* on cruises out on Inverness. She operated in Orkney waters in the winter months and she was moved to the Clyde to offer short cruises from Helensburgh for one summer season in 1967.

Below: Jessie Ellen at Muirtown Locks on 31 July 1961. In 1970 she was sold for use on Loch Etive. (G.E. Langmuir Collection, Mitchell Library, Glasgow)

Jacobite Cruises commenced operation in 1975 with *Jacobite Princess*. *Jacobite Chieftain* and *Jacobite Clansman* were purchased in 1976, having previously been *Bosun's Sue* and *Bosun's Jane* respectively at York. *Jacobite Lady* was a larger, two-decked vessel, which was built in 1975 and also entered service in 1976. Initially two vessels ran out of Inverness and two out of Fort William for a season in 1976, but the Fort William sailings ceased after that season. *Jacobite Chieftain* became *Lomond Chieftain* operating out of Tarbet in 1987 and *Jacobite Clansman* became *Lochaber Lady* at Fort William and then the second *Lomond Queen* on Loch Lomond in 1988. *Jacobite Lady* was also sold to Cruise Loch Lomond after the 1989 season, and became their *Lomond Laird*. *Jacobite Princess*, which had opened the service in 1975, was sold to the other end of Loch Ness and ran for a spell as *Abbey Princess* out of Fort Augustus. *Jacobite Chieftain* is shown in this picture with *Jacobite Lady* and *Jacobite Clansman* in 1981.

In 1987 the first *Lomond Queen* was purchased and became the first *Jacobite Queen*. In 1988 the former Tyne ferry *Tyne Queen*, which was built in 1949, was purchased. She was extensively converted at Ardmaleish on Bute for the Loch Ness service, with a funnel being added. Then she became the second *Jacobite Queen*, so the first vessel of that name was renamed *Jacobite Warrior*. The popularity of monster-spotting trips has ensured the popularity of the Jacobite Cruises operation, which incorporates a call at Urquhart Castle and round trips on bus and boat. From the winter of 2003/04 the 100-passenger vessel *Jacobite Spirit* joined the fleet, and cruises are now offered all the year round, both from Tomnahurich Bridge, Inverness, and from the Clansman Hotel, Drumnadrochit. At the time of writing it is not clear if this is a newly-built vessel or if it has been purchased second-hand.

Above: Royal Scot, operated by Cruise Loch Ness, is one of a number of small vessels which have given Loch Ness cruises out of Fort Augustus in the past two decades. This picture of her was taken on 1 July 1991.

Right: Caledonian Queen, which was operated by Loch Ness Cruises, also operated out of Fort Augustus, as shown by this 1983 handbill.

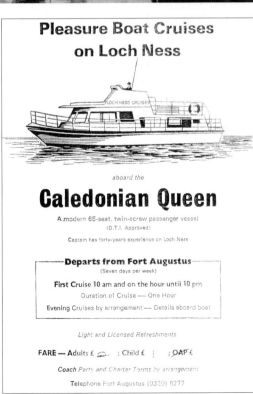

Pleasure Boat Cruises on Loch Ness

aboard the

Caledonian Queen

A modern 65-seat, twin-screw passenger vessel
(D.T.I. Approved)

Captain has forty-years experience on Loch Ness

Departs from Fort Augustus
(Seven days per week)

First Cruise 10 am and on the hour until 10 pm
Duration of Cruise —— One Hour

Evening Cruises by arrangement —— Details aboard boat

Light and Licensed Refreshments

FARE — Adults £ ⌐ ; Child £ | ; OAP £

Coach Party and Charter Terms by arrangement

Telephone Fort Augustus (0320) 6277

Neptune's Lady was a former Dutch vessel which ran out of Banavie in 1988 and out of Fort Augustus in 1989. She was built as a steam tug in 1908 and later saw service for Rotterdam excursion operator Spido as *Regentesseplaat*. At Groningen she became a floating pub, named *Regentesse*. Around 1990 she was moved to Glasgow and since then has been moored at Windmillcroft Quay, just downriver from the former Bridge Wharf, at the premises of Euroyachts.

The Kyle to Kyleakin ferry *Lochalsh* of 1951 was sold in 1958 to the British Waterways Board for use as a crane barge. She is seen here at Banavie in 1989.

nine

The Forth and Clyde Canal and the Union Canal

From top:

On 28 March 1803 the first commercial steamboat in Europe, Symington's *Charlotte Dundas*, ran on the Forth and Clyde Canal as a tug. She towed two barges from Lock 20 at Wyndford to Port Dundas. She was subsequently forbidden to ply on the canal due to allegations about excess wash causin damage to the canal banks, and was laid up until she sank in 1808.

In the late 1980s a three-quarter-scale replica of *Charlotte Dundas* was built at Cockenzie for Falkirk district council. Unfortunately the project leader died before the engine could be completed, and it was not until 2003 that the replica was fully complete, being restored at the Arbroath shipyard shown here. She is now on the Forth and Clyde Canal at the Falkirk Wheel.

A model of *Charlotte Dundas*, showing the trough-mounted stern wheel.

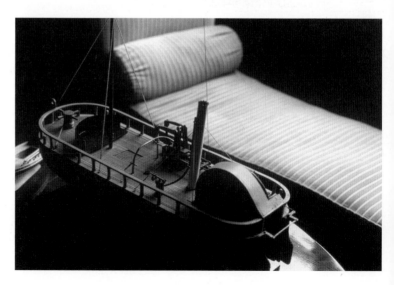

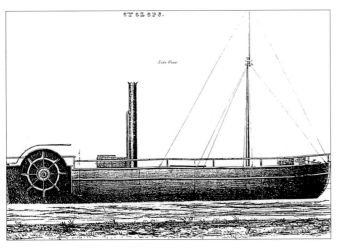

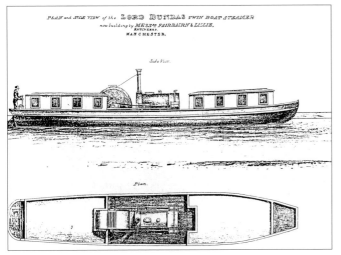

From top:

In 1829, *Cyclops*, which had been built in 1824 as a horse-drawn boat, was converted to steam with a single cylinder engine and a stern wheel. She ran from Port Dundas to Alloa, carrying cargo and fifteen passengers.

In 1831, a second steamer named *Lord Dundas* entered service for passengers from Port Dundas to Lock 16. She had a two-cylinder horizontal engine and a mid-mounted paddle wheel. She was built in Manchester by Fairbairn and Lilley and sailed to the Clyde. It is said she was the first iron-hulled steamer to sail on the open sea. She was followed by the larger stern-wheeled *Manchester*, from the same builders, which ran to Stirling. *Lord Dundas* had ceased running by 1838, but *Manchester* and *Cyclops* remained in service until around 1844.

Rockvilla Castle was built in 1859 by T. Wingate & Co. and had an unusual machinery arrangement of a three-cylinder oscillating engine. She ran from Port Dundas to Lock 16 at Falkirk. In 1875 she came into the ownership of George Aitken, who was also her captain, and from then on ran only as far as Castlecary, but continuing to Lock 16 on Sundays. She was, in effect, a steam-driven version of the *Swift* horse-drawn boats, which provided passenger services on the canal at that time. On 7 April 1880, George Aitken fell overboard and was drowned. *Rockvilla Castle* was taken over by James Glover of Paisley, who ran her until the end of the 1881 season, when it is believed she was scrapped at Paisley. (G.E. Langmuir Collection, Mitchell Library, Glasgow)

From top:

In 1893, George Aitken's son James founded the firm of James Aitken & Co. and ordered a new steamer for the canal from John H. Gilmour & Co. of Irvine, to be named *Fairy Queen*. She was based at Kirkintilloch and ran from Port Dundas to Craigmarloch. She was sold in March 1897 to the Shannon Development Co. of Dublin. She ran on the Shannon until 1906, retaining her name, and was then moved to Lough Corrib, from Galway to Cong, where she ran until 1913. She was then sold back to the Glasgow shipbroker Walter Fulton, although she was still registered at Dublin. She remained in the Mercantile navy list until 1935. Photographs show her operating on the Tyne. She is seen here on the Shannon. (G.E. Langmuir Collection, Mitchell Library, Glasgow)

The V-shaped compound diagonal machinery fitted to the first *Fairy Queen* was built by Hall-Brown, Buttery & Co. of Govan. (G.E. Langmuir Collection, Mitchell Library, Glasgow)

The timetable for the Forth and Clyde Canal service of the first *Fairy Queen* in 1894. (G.E. Langmuir Collection, Mitchell Library, Glasgow)

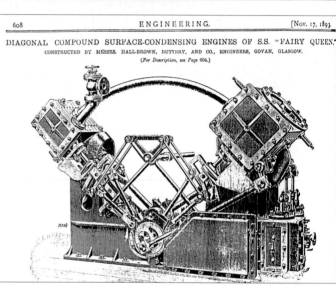

608   ENGINEERING.   [Nov. 17, 1893.

DIAGONAL COMPOUND SURFACE-CONDENSING ENGINES OF S.S. "FAIRY QUEEN."
CONSTRUCTED BY MESSRS. HALL-BROWN, BUTTERY, AND CO., ENGINEERS, GOVAN, GLASGOW.
(For Description, see Page 604.)

The "Fairy Queen" Route.

HOURS OF SAILING.

CRAIGMARLOCH TO GLASGOW.				GLASGOW TO CRAIGMARLOCH.		
Leaving	Morning.	After-noon.	Even-ing.	Leaving	Morning.	After-noon.
Craigmarloch, -	...	1.10	7.5	Port Dundas, - -	10	4.15
Auchinstarry, -	...	1.20	7.15	Rockvilla, - -	10.5	4.20
Twechar, -	...	1.40	7.35	Ruchill Bridge,- -	10.20	4.35
Kirkintilloch, -	8	2.20	8.10	Lambhill, - -	10.35	4.50
Torrance, -	8.20	2.40	...	Farm Bridge, - -	11	5.15
Cadder, -	8.30	2.50	...	Cadder, - -	11.10	5.25
Farm Bridge, -	8.40	3	...	Torrance, - -	11.15	5.30
Lambhill, -	9	3.20	...	Kirkintilloch, - -	11.45	6
Ruchill, -	9.25	3.45	...	Twechar, - -	12.15	6.30
Rockvilla, -	9.40	4	...	Auchinstarry, -	12.35	6.50
Port Dundas, -	9.45	4.5	...	Craigmarloch, -	12.50	7

For any alterations during the season see newspaper advts. and diaries.

Single Fare to Kirkintilloch, 6d.; to Craigmarloch, 9d.

In 1897 a second *Fairy Queen* was built, this time by McArthur & Co. of Paisley, with a vertical engine by Bow McLachlan of Paisley. She was larger than her predecessor and was based at Port Dundas rather than at Kirkintilloch. After *Gipsy Queen* was introduced in 1905, she was used mainly for charter traffic and was sold to the Tyneside shipbuilders Hawthorn Leslie for Tyne ferry service in 1912. In 1940 she was sold to Seaham Harbour Trust, and was broken up in 1947. (G.E. Langmuir Collection, Mitchell Library, Glasgow)

1903 saw the entry into service of *May Queen,* which was a consort for *Fairy Queen*. She was built at Kirkintilloch at the yard of Peter McGregor. She sailed on a new afternoon return service from Port Dundas to Kirkintilloch. At the end of 1917 she was sold to Palmer's Shipbuilding and Iron Company of Hebburn-on-Tyne. She was sold again around 1936 to the Millom and Askam Hematite Iron Co. Ltd of Millom in Cumberland.

19/9/1904

IDEAL AUTUMN SAILING TILL 26th SEPT.

S. S. FAIRY QUEEN and MAY QUEEN. Daily (except Saturday) from Port-Dundas (near Cowcaddens), at 10 a.m., for Kirkintilloch (Return Fare, 1s) and Craigmarloch (Return Fare, 1s 6d). Back in City at 4.50.

The NEW SELECT AFTERNOON SAIL leaving at 2.15. Back in City at 6.15. Return Fare, 1s.

NOTE—Saturday Sailings on 17th and 24th September at 10 a.m. for Kirkintilloch; at 2.15 and 3 p.m. for Kirkintilloch and Craigmarloch.

An advertisement for 19 September 1904, for the cruises by *Fairy Queen* and *May Queen*.

In 1904 a competitor arrived with the steamer *Truro Belle*, bearing the Lochgoil funnel colours of red with two white bands and a black top. She had been built in 1895 at Dartmouth for excursions on the River Fal from Falmouth to Truro, and was sold in about 1898 to Sunderland owners for use as a Tyne ferry. Her spell on the canal was short and she was taken over by the Bank of Scotland before the end of the season, and sold by them to a Dundee owner in March 1905. She was broken up in 1907. (G.E. Langmuir Collection, Mitchell Library, Glasgow)

Gipsy Queen was built by Bow McLachlan of Paisley for James Aitken, and entered service in May 1905. She is pictured here at Cadder. She was completely different from the earlier steamers, with a much more modern appearance.

Gipsy Queen at Hillhead in Kirkintilloch. She and *May Queen* continued sailing throughout the First World War.

A BONNIE VIEW NEAR HILLHEAD, KIRKINTILLOCH.   A 5901.

Gipsy Queen again at Hillhead in Kirkintilloch with a couple of ramblers who are on the towpath. Children would run along the towpath, hoping to catch coins thrown by the passengers.

GIPSY QUEEN AT SHIRVA.

Gipsy Queen at Shirva, which is a couple of miles east of Kirkintilloch. James Aitken, who had been both owner and captain, retired in 1929 and the company was taken over by his son George.

ON THE CANAL, CRAIGMARLOCH.

Gipsy Queen at the end of her journey at Craigmarloch, which is now a suburb of Cumbernauld. *Gipsy Queen* was withdrawn shortly after the outbreak of war in September 1939, and was scrapped in the June of the following year at Bowling.

22/8/'923

ACROSS SCOTLAND.
CHARMING INLAND SAILS.
Fine Saloon Steamer "GIPSY QUEEN."
From PORT-DUNDAS DAILY (ex. Sat.)
(Cars to Normal School, New City Road.)
10 a.m. for CRAIGMARLOCH ....Return, 2s 6d
Or All-Day Sail, Dinner and Tea 5s 9d
SATURDAY SAILS.—At 2.15 p.m. for CRAIG-
MARLOCH ....Return 2s 6d
EVENING CRUISE—Tuesdays, at 6.30 p.m.
Return Fare 1s 4d

AFTERNOON NEW MOTOR SAILS.
To CRAIGMARLOCH per M.S. "FAIRY QUEEN."
Daily, (except Saturday), at 2.15 p.m.
Return Fares, 2s 6d .... With Tea, 3s 9d.
About 2 Hours Ashore. Back, 8.15 p.m
Day and Evening Cruise Parties Booked.—Terms:—
JAMES AITKEN & CO., LTD., KIRKINTILLOCH.

A 22 August 1923 advertisement for *Gipsy Queen*. The fares are cheap: 2s 6d for a whole day's sail, or 5s 9d including meals. These included lunch at Craigmarloch, in the restaurant known as The Bungalow. There was also a floating tea room, named *Meadow Queen*, and recreation grounds. The new *Fairy Queen* is also featured.

In 1923, the third *Fairy Queen* was built, a small motor vessel built by Hugh McLean & Sons Ltd of Renfrew, seen here at Port Dundas. She was sold in 1931 to an owner at Warrenpoint for use on Carlingford Lough. (G.E. Langmuir Collection, Mitchell Library, Glasgow)

On 12 October 1962 the CSP's motor vessel *Ashton* made a trip from Bowling to Kirkintilloch on charter to the Glasgow University Railway Society. On this trip she stopped at Knightswood to free a wire that had been caught round her propellor. Two months later the canal was closed.

In 1995 the Clyde River Steamer Club operated *The Second Snark* on a charter. It went into the Bowling Basin, which had remained open when the rest of the canal was closed.

****

M.V. FERRY QUEEN now sails from

GLASGOW ROAD BRIDGE

(on the A803 Glasgow to Kirkintilloch road by The Stables Restaurant)

SATURDAY AND SUNDAY AFTERNOONS

at 1.30 and 3.30 and Public Holiday Monday afternoons

FARES: Adults £1.50   Children 50p
Society Members, O.A.Ps. and Unwaged £1.00

The trip takes approximately one and a half hours

****

How to get there --

BY CAR -Take the A803 Bishopbriggs to Kirkintilloch road and look out for
The Stables Licensed Restaurant, Car Parking available.

BY BUS -There is a frequent service of Midland Scottish buses from Buchanan
Street Bus Station- Stances No. 8 to 12.

THE FERRY QUEEN can be chartered for parties of up to 60
passengers. Ask for a leaflet or phone 041-776 0017 (Daytime) or
041-776 3812 (Evening) for details.

In 1980 the Forth and Clyde Canal Society was formed to stimulate the revival of the canal. The revival came to full fruition in the Millennium Link Project, and saw the full reopening of the canal in 2001 and the opening of the Falkirk Wheel, which connects it with the Union Canal in 2002. In 1980 the Forth and Clyde Canal Society purchased two former Clyde Navigation Trust passenger ferries: *Ferry No. 2* (1934) and *Ferry No. 8* (1951). The former was never used, but the latter was converted into the trip boat *Ferry Queen,* which offered cruises from the Stables Inn, a mile or so west of Kirkintilloch, towards Cadder.

Above: Ferry Queen on a Paddle Steamer Preservation Society charter in 1986. She continued operating on the canal for almost two decades.

Left: Ferry Queen turning in mid-canal at Cadder on the same occasion as the previous picture. She brought back the 'Lochgoil' funnel colours, which had been used on *Truro Belle*.

Ferry Queen was withdrawn in 1998 and sold to the Clyde Maritime Trust the following year. In 2002 she was moved back to the Clyde and is seen here in summer 2003 berthed alongside the sailing ship *Glenlee* with her former name, *Ferry No. 8*, restored.

Another Clyde ferry, *Ferry No. 10* (1934), also made her way to the canal. She was extensively altered and fitted with an outboard motor. She was named *Caledonian* and ran as a restaurant boat from The Stables Inn. *Caledonian* was withdrawn in around 2002 and is now in static use as a floating craft studio, known as *Craft Daft on a Raft*, and moored at The Stables.

In 1987 *Lady Margaret* was built as a restaurant boat for use on the canal for Scotland in View, which was owned by Commander Patrick Le Pla. She ceased operating in around 1999, and was sold to British Waterways who renamed her *Millennium Link*. She is used by them as a VIP launch and is based at the Falkirk Wheel.

Gipsy Princess was built in 1990 for the Forth and Clyde Canal Society, and is pictured here at Auchinstarry, which is south of Kilsyth. She operates weekend trips from here.

Above: The Forth and Clyde Canal Society also owns *Janet Telford*, which is again seen at Auchinstarry. She was built in the 1980s for the Seagull Trust, who cater for disabled groups. They have a large fleet of craft on the Forth and Clyde and Union Canals. *Janet Telford* was purchased by the society in 1994.

Right: The Monkland Canal, which ran from Port Dundas to Coatbridge and Airdrie, was closed in around 1935. Most of it was filled in in the 1950s, but a small stretch remains close to the Summerlee Industrial Museum at Coatbridge. The small steam launch *Fire Queen* occasionally sails on this and is seen here outside the museum.

The Falkirk Wheel is a unique piece of engineering which is designed to transport boats up from the level of the Forth and Clyde Canal to the Union Canal, which is some 115ft higher. A flight of locks further east originally accomplished this, but these were filled in in 1933.

A small fleet of boats offer trips up and down the wheel from the visitor centre at the bottom, which is seen in the background here. These include *Shanks First*, *Forth and Clyde* and *Union*. The wooden Norfolk Broads launch *Princess Mary* arrived in 2003.

The Linlithgow Union Canal Society established a small museum at Linlithgow in 1976. Since then, they have operated the small pseudo-antique steam profile launch *Victoria* on short trips from there.

In 1995 the society purchased the larger *Saint Magdalene*, which was built in 1990 as *Ohmega* for use on the Monmouth and Brecon Canal. She runs longer cruises to the Avon Aqueduct and monthly trips to the Falkirk Wheel.

In 1974 the landlord of the Ratho Inn on the Union Canal, Ronnie Rusack, started the revival of the Union Canal. Cruises went from there to the Almond Aqueduct on the newly-built restaurant boat *Pride of the Union*, which is seen here at Ratho.

In around 1988, a second restaurant boat, *Pride of Belhaven*, was purchased. She was originally named *Thomas Skipwith*, and operated on the River Soar at Sileby near Loughborough. She is pictured at a photograph stop on the Almond Aqueduct.

With the re-opening of the full length of the canal, cruises through to Edinburgh have been made possible, and in the other direction to Linlithgow and beyond. *Pride of Belhaven* is seen here at Linlithgow on the occasion of a Coastal Cruising Association charter in May 2001. In 2003 she operated occasional Edinburgh to Glasgow excursions, with passengers staying overnight on land.

In 1994 the former Norfolk Broads wooden launch *Ratho Princess* was introduced. She was built in 1921 as *Prince*, and is seen here on the Almond Aqueduct. She makes regular trips from Ratho to here.

An advertising postcard shows the three members of the fleet operated by the Bridge Inn in Ratho.

The Seagull Trust commenced operations out of Ratho in 1979 with *St John Crusader*, which is in the background here. In 1985 *MacKay Seagull*, pictured here in the foreground, joined her. Later *St John Crusader II* was built. All the vessels operated by the Seagull Trust are specially designed to cater for groups of the disabled. *Govan Seagull* was built by Govan Shipbuilders in 1984, and operates out of Falkirk on the Union Canal. *Yarrow Seagull* was built in 1983 by the apprentices of Yarrow Shipbuilders, and operates out of Kirkintilloch on the Forth and Clyde Canal. *Highland Seagull* was built in 1989, and operates on the Caledonian Canal, from Tomnahurich Bridge in Inverness.

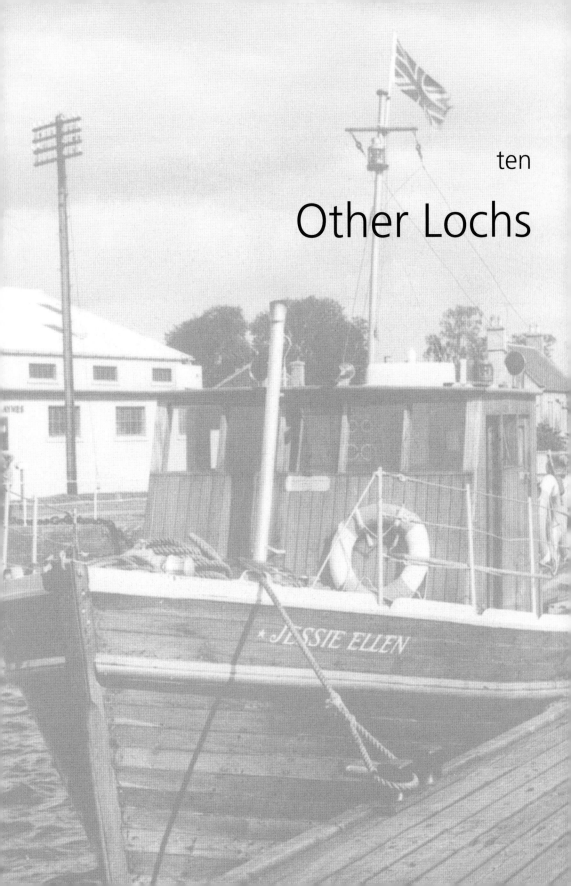

ten

Other Lochs

Lake of Menteith: A small steam launch, which was possibly named *Mary*, ran on the Lake of Menteith to Inchmahome Priory until 1901. The Lake of Menteith is the only body of water in Scotland known as a lake rather than a loch. The motor vessel *The MacGregor* ran from 1902 until the time of the First World War, and small open motorboats have operated the service since then. *The MacGregor* is pictured. (G.E. Langmuir Collection, Mitchell Library, Glasgow)

Lanark Loch: An unnamed steam launch ran on Lanark Loch in the early years of the twentieth century. She is seen here in a postcard view, which is postmarked 16 June 1916.

Loch Arkaig: The small steam launch *The Rifle* ran a mail and supply service on Loch Arkaig from 1861 until 1939. She was owned by clan chief Cameron of Lochiel, and also carried his guests on shooting trips. She carried Queen Victoria in 1873 and the Duke of York in the 1930s. *The Rifle* also occasionally towed timber barges. (Douglas Brown Collection)

The Rifle was sold for scrapping in 1939 and was sunk while this was being undertaken. Her remains were raised in 1990 by a recovery vehicle from Spean Bridge Garage, and were taken to the Scottish Maritime Museum at Irvine, where she lies at the time of writing, awaiting restoration.

Loch Earn: The motor vessel *Queen of Loch Earn* was built in 1922 at Fraserburgh for Peter Crerar of Crieff, who was a bus operator. She ran in connection with his bus tours. In 1928 he sold out to the Scottish General Omnibus Co. Ltd, who in turn were taken over in 1930 by W. Alexander & Sons Ltd of Falkirk, who preferred to use their own coaches on the road alongside Loch Earn, so she was withdrawn after the 1936 season and was initially sold to a scrap merchant. He sold her on for use as a houseboat named *Earnhull*. She lay on the shore opposite St Fillans for many years.

Left: Maid of the Loch was a small eight-passenger electric boat used on Loch Earn in the 1980s.

Below: Loch Eck: The first steamer on Loch Eck was *Aglaia*, which was introduced by David Napier in around 1820. She was the first iron passenger steamer in the world, and a steam carriage initially ran from Kilmun to the foot of the loch in connection with her sailings. A horse-drawn coach soon replaced this after it proved too heavy for the road. *Aglaia* was reportedly maliciously scuttled and was replaced by another small paddle steamer in 1828. The steamer service lapsed some time after that. It was revived in 1878 by *Fairy Queen*, which was built by T.B. Seath & Co. of Rutherglen, with a two-cylinder simple expansion engine by A. Campbell & Co. of Glasgow. She was built for the owners of the Glasgow to Inveraray steamer, *Lord of the Isles*, and is seen here with a grey hull.

Fairy Queen at the head of the loch, with the connecting coaches for Strachur.

Fairy Queen at Inverchapel, at the foot of the loch.

This is a night view of *Fairy Queen* in grey-hulled condition. She ceased operation in 1914 at the outbreak of the First World War, and resumed sailing in 1919. She was withdrawn in 1926 and scrapped. The Loch Eck tour was then undertaken by a motorbus from Dunoon to Strachur, and to Inveraray after the closure of Strachur pier in 1935.

Loch Maree: *Mabel* was initially owned by the owner of the Loch Maree Hotel, but was purchased in 1887 by David MacBrayne. She had been built in 1882 by T.B. Seath & Co. of Rutherglen, and ran from Tollie to the head of the loch at Rudha 'n Fhomhair. She was withdrawn after the 1911 season and lay on the beach near the Loch Maree Hotel until at least 1937. After her withdrawal, a motorboat service operated on the loch for a year or two.

Loch Ossian: The steamer *Cailleach* was launched in 1902 for service on this isolated loch near Corrour station. R. McAllister of Dumbarton was her builder, with engines by Matthew Paul & Co. She ran from near the present-day youth hostel to Corrour Lodge, which was a shooting lodge at the far end of the loch. It was owned by Sir John Stirling Maxwell, of Pollok House in Glasgow, who is seen in the background of this photograph. She was withdrawn in the early 1930s and was sold for transfer by rail to an owner in Morar or Arisaig.

Loch Rannoch: The steamer *Gitana* was built for service on Loch Rannoch by T.B. Seath & Co. in June 1881. On 6 February 1882 she sank at her moorings in a storm. (G.E. Langmuir Collection, Mitchell Library, Glasgow)

Around 1972 *Gitana* was raised from the bed of the loch, and was prepared for preservation and a return to service. Her engine was overhauled and a wooden enclosed upper deck was fitted. However, in November 1983, a storm again arose and her mooring parted. *Gitana* at that time had the misfortune to be driven ashore where her hull disintegrated. (G.E. Langmuir Collection, Mitchell Library, Glasgow)

Loch Treig: The puffer *Loch Treig* was used here in 1894 during the construction of the West Highland Railway. H. Robb of Leith had built her. (G.E. Langmuir Collection, Mitchell Library, Glasgow)

Glasgow, Paisley and Johnstone Canal: This canal was almost entirely served by horse-drawn craft, but a steamer was tried on one occasion, variously quoted as 1840 and 1870. Reputedly the canal was so shallow that it dug up the canal bed and the experiment was not repeated. This view is taken at the Blackhall Viaduct over the River Cart at Hawkhead, Paisley. The canal was closed in 1881 and its course utilised for a railway line by the Glasgow and South Western Railway. (Renfrewshire Libraries)

River Ythan: The paddle tug *Despatch* was used on the river Ythan. It towed barges from the port of Newburgh to Ellon from 1874 until 1924. (J&C McCutcheon collection)

Other local titles published by Tempus

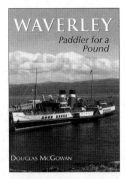

Waverley Paddler for a pound
DOUGLAS MCGOWAN

In the early 1970s an outdated mode of transport was about to disappear forever with the retirement of PS *Waverley*, the last Clyde Coast paddle steamer. For over a hundred years, paddlers had puffed their way 'doon the watter'. In 1974, Douglas McGowan purchased *Waverley* for the princely sum of £1. Lovingly restored, she has been a regular visitor at ports all around the British coast and has travelled far and wide.
0 7524 2877 2

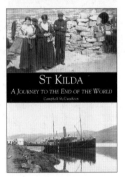

St Kilda A Journey to the End of the World
CAMPBELL MCCUTCHEON

At the far-flung western corner of the British Isles is a group of islands called St Kilda, famous for being the remotest inhabited part of Britain. Countless tourists have visited this World Heritage Site over the past 300 years. Evacuated in 1930, the island has been uninhabited since, save for an army base and thousands of birds, some unique to the island. This is the tale of a tour by the SS *Hebrides* from Glasgow to the 'island at the end of the world'.
0 7524 2380 0

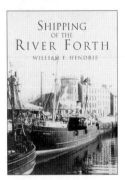

Shipping of the River Forth
WILLIAM F. HENDRIE

Within the pages of *Shipping of the River Forth* are views of long-gone ships, the fishing industry, coasters and ocean liners as well as paddle steamers, shipwrecks and the people involved in maritime industries along both banks of the river.

0 7524 2117 4

Caledonian Steam Packet Company Ltd
ALISTAIR DEAYTON

In *Caledonian Steam Packet Company Ltd* Alistair Deayton tells the story of this shipping company and the ships that served it. It still survives today after its 1970s amalgamation with David MacBrayne to become Caledonian MacBryane, the Scottish island ferry company. Profusely illustrated with over 250 illustrations of the ships and the ports, piers and harbours they served, this is the definitive illustrated history of this famous company.
0 7524 2381 9

If you are interested in purchasing other books published by Tempus, or in case you have difficulty finding any Tempus books in your local bookshop, you can also place orders directly through our website

www.tempus-publishing.com

or from   BOOKPOST, Freepost, PO Box 29, Douglas, Isle of Man, IM99 1BQ
tel 01624 836000   email bookshop@enterprise.net